Boy from th

By

Terry L. Weldon

"Boy"

I dedicate this book to my family, both immediate and extended. They inspired me to write it in order to pass on the tales of growing up at a time when we weren't controlled by technology and political correctness in a part of the United States where family values were still important.

My Beasley roots...

My name is Terry Weldon and my fondest memories from childhood is my relationship with my grandparents, P.O. and Dollie Beasley. They raised me from the time I was 4 years old until I left home at 18. They were poor by all economic standards, but, they were family-oriented people who lived the only way they knew how with strong family vlues. The doors to their home were never locked so brothers and sisters, sons and daughters, grandchildren and cousins, nieces and nephews were always welcomed anytime day or night.

Although Granny Beasley worked the farm with Grandpa P.O., she managed to make time for the children, and the grandchildren. Granny, herself was the baby of eleven, all of which survived to adulthood, with several of them living into their 90's and even 100. She, herself lived to see almost 92 years old, while God saw fit to take Grandpa home to heaven in his sixties. They were married in the 1920s and had eleven kids of their own. It was just natural for them to be surrounded by children. I suppose because she grew up with ten siblings, she just assumed you were supposed to have eleven kids.

We lived in the same little farm house in the edge of a cotton field just outside of Gideon Missouri as far back as I can remember. The town's ballpark was out in the country away from town across the road from our house and on warm summer nights, if I wasn't over there playing ball, we would sit with the windows open and listen to the sounds of summer. These were quite times when we would just listen to the game and not really saying anything to each other another. Otherwise, we were glued to the Television screen like most families of the late fifties and early sixties. We could get 2 channels o.k. and a third one on clear nights. There was no need for a TV guide. I had all seven days per week memorized.

Now days when I smell cotton being ginned or a summer rain, it takes me right back to my Grandpa and Granny Beasley and that little house out by the ball diamond.

Granny Beasley was the kindest woman I have ever known. I liked to think she never spanked me because I was such a fine young man, but in later years I realized, it was because she didn't have a cruel bone in her body. I just happen to benefit from that character trait, and I am glad for it. She took care of her sister's children even when she was a young girl herself. She was very close to her family (the Parr family) throughout her lifetime. I can remember her brothers, sisters, nieces and nephews visiting from Alabama and Arkansas on a regular basis and we would go there as often as we could. I'm sure she had her days when nothing went right, but I never saw one in my lifetime. Even when Grandpa P.O. would come home Saturday evening a "little under the weather", she scoffed at him a little and went on back to quilting. Most of my generation owns and cherishes a "Granny Quilt". She tried, and may have succeeded, in making one for everyone in the family. I and my three children each have one. She so loved the family reunion we have every year, where we camp for 3-4 days in the foothills of Southeast Missouri. She would start a couple of months earlier saying she didn't think she was going to make it this year, that it was too hard on her, however she was usually in one of the first few vehicles to take off for the campground every year. She was there when she was 92.

As I said earlier Granny Beasley was fortunate enough to have had eleven children. All were perfectly normal human beings with the exception of one which was severely handicapped. Granny took care of Little Bill at home until he got to be too strong for her to physically handle. They regretfully placed in an institution. I can remember her crying half way back home after visiting him. She did her very best to care for him and never stopped trying until she finally had him relocated to a nursing home closer to her until he passed away. She always felt bad about Little Bill's situation, but I know God was proud of her for her devotion to one of his special children.

Granny made her mark on everyone in the family with one simple little phrase, "Who's that-a-comin'?". When visitors came to our home, she would meet them at the door with a smile and a "Who's that-a-comin'?". I'm sure that everyone in the family that knew Granny Beasley has stepped to their own door at home and said those simple words that mean so much to us all.

Grandpa P.O. worked every day from sunrise til 5:00pm, because that is when the box plant whistle blew in our hometown of Gideon, Missouri and the Little Rascals came on channel 6 out of Paducah Kentucky. Saturday he worked half a day and was usually "under the influence" by 2:00pm. Sunday morning he was up at the same time as he was everyday, around 5:30am, however, his sole purpose in life was to get the "kids" to come to Sunday dinner. He had Granny cooking by 6:30 and me on the telephone trying to convince them they should come and eat with us. I do not remember to this day if we were ever turned down. Granny cooked enough for a small army and Aunt Peg, Aunt Jewell, Aunt Deaner, Aunt Jean, and Aunt Pauline came with arms loaded with food. Sometimes we would have a treat and Uncle Leon and Aunt Leona would come to spend the day. On a typical Sunday, in and around this small farmhouse in Southeast Missouri you could count somewhere in the neighborhood of 35 to 40 people, and on Holidays or days when my Uncle Smokey would come home from the service, that little house would swell to busting.

Like I said, Grandpa P.O. worked on the farm almost everyday and and spent very little time with his children, however, on the weekends, he found the time to play with the Grandchildren, the more, the merrier. He loved to torment them until he had half of them crying and the other half so wound up, their parents couldn't do anything with them. I believe that's just the way he liked it! He never got to enjoy our family reunions, but I am sure that he would have been the first to go and the last to leave had he lived long enough to go.

He made his sons work in the fields with him as they were growing up to help feed the family, but by the time I came along his attitude had changed a little. His sons weren't allowed to play ball because they had to chop or pick cotton. He let me play ball and work in the field after practice. I told my uncles, "The man that raised you is not the same man that raised me". Because farming is such a hit and miss business, Grandpa P.O. was also a master handyman. He would build porches, add rooms, and do some roofing to supplement his farming income. When I got old enough to help, I found myself on the rooftops of most houses in Gideon Missouri. Then after a while he would get the jobs started and I would finish them. It was his way of teaching me a trade and getting me spending money that he didn't really have.

I can't talk about Grandpa P.O. without talking about pocket knives. For some unknown reason to me, his generation was fascinated with pocket knives. In order to be a true knife swapper, you had to have at least one in your pocket to trade. Plus one that was razor sharp. He would sit with "his generation" on the benches in front of Gibb's tavern and the Commercial bank of Gideon every Saturday afternoon and see who could get their knife the sharpest. Most of them had no hair on their arms from demonstrating how sharp their knives were. My generation called in "spit and whittle corner". Funny how each generation passes the time.

Saturdays, Grandpa P.O. would come in at noon from the field and change from dirty overalls to clean overalls, than come out on the front porch where I had the water, soap and razor ready. I would shave him and he would give me fifty cents spending money. That got me into the Malden theater to see a double feature, popcorn and a soda. (Try that now). I still have that shaving mug. I suppose it is my way of hanging on to a little piece of him. My cousin Danny is the lucky one, he got Grandpa P.O.'s last pocket knife. That is a treasure. I often wondered what our lives would have been like had Grandpa P.O. lived longer. I know they would have been better for it. He really wasn't a steady church-going man, but I know he had a relationship with God in his own way. I still miss him.

It's a rare day that I am not reminded of them both because there are so many things they shared with me. Granny loved making quilts, putting together puzzles, playing dominos and sitting on the front porch swing and watching life go by. I'd sit at the kitchen table and listen to her talk while she folded and patted a dish towel until it was perfectly square. In my younger days I remember riding the tractor with Grandpa P.O. for hours on end. He always had a nickel or two in his pocket for me, although he didn't really have many stories to tell, it wasn't really his stories I was looking for, it was his company I always treasured most.

So many small traditions, foods, interests, and memories came from that little farm house just outside of Gideon Missouri they shared with all of us. But when you add them all up, what they truly gave us was their limited time, and a legacy of love: a rich heritage of family life to pass down from generations before. It has been forty-six years since we shared that time together, I still miss them both like it was yesterday.

"How do you get a sweet little 80-year-old lady to say the F word;

You get another sweet little 80-year-old lady to yell (BINGO!)"
anonymous

Yule Log Christmas...

In the late 1800s, W.T. Chesser and his family settled a small island on the eastern edge of the Okefenokee Swamp. The Chesser's were a rugged family, carving out a life in the often harsh conditions of the area. Their history is typical of many area settlers; they ate what they could shoot, trap, catch and grow on the sandy soil of the swamp. They lived simply, worked hard, and played hard, when possible. He settled the area currently known as Chesser Island, filled with forest in the low areas of the swamp. Every year since moving to Florida, my cousins, Jackie and Linda Carol "Beasley" had talked of going the Old Chesser Homestead to enjoy the Yule Log Christmas celebration they presented each year. After their trip there the local newspaper had an article about how wonderful the event was that year. There was a picture of Jackie, Linda Carol, Jackie's daughter Shari and her two daughters, Kara and Kelli setting around the campfire laughing and having a great time enjoying the Yule Log celebration. The article talked about how beautifully decorated the old homestead was in the time period of days gone by, about the wonderful play that was presented to all of the guests depicting the life and times of the Chesser family. It told of the hot chocolate and cute little squirrel cookies provided. It sounded like such a wonderful holiday event.

Well, the following is their memories of this special adventure to the Yule log Celebration at the Okefenokee Swamp. It began when they got to the parking area and discovered the parking area was about a quarter of a mile from the sandy path leading to the Chesser Homestead. Remember, this in the middle of the swamp with absolutely no lights. There was no moon out that night and they had brought no flashlights. Just when they managed to make it to the path, they saw a hayride wagon waiting. Tired and frustrated by the unexpected hike through the swamp, they all decided it would be fun to take a hayride and do some Caroling to start the fun before continuing on their adventure. They hadn't travelled very far when they came upon some cars parked blocking the hayride wagon. The wagon could neither get through nor turn around. They had no choice but to abandon the idea of a Christmas hayride with caroling. They got off of the wagon and along with ten strangers, stumbled their way to the Chesser homestead to see all of the decorations. Arriving at the Chesser Homestead and to their surprise, were two sprigs of evergreen on the fireplace mantel and a tree with a few kernels of popcorn on it. Not being discouraged, they heard the play was about to start so they hurried outside to find a good place to sit and watch the play. There were several other people there and they had taken the "good" seats so they sort of settled on the side of the yard which prevented Kara from seeing the actors. Linda Carol decided to take Kara and walk around to the front for her to get a better view and enjoy the presentation. It was a depiction of the Chesser Family's first Christmas's.

The women were cooking and children playing etc. Suddenly Linda and Kara heard this LOUD voice that sounded mighty familiar to them. It was Jackie saying in her best "teacher" voice, "BOYS please settle down, we are trying to hear the play!" What Jackie didn't know was those boys were part of the play! Trying her best to keep anyone from being embarrassed, Linda Carol sent Kara, back around to tell her MaMa that the boys were part of the play! After Jackie stop scolding the boys, they were able to finish the play.

When the play was over they decided to get some hot chocolate and cookies to sip and eat around the Yule Log fire. When they got back inside to the table, there was only one cup of chocolate left and three cookies that were so hard they couldn't break them to share them. Failing to get the cocoa and cookies, they moved on the Yule log fire. They were able to find a log to sit on while the girls played in the sand waiting for the caroling to begin around the Yule Log Fire. They waited and waited at least an hour and had just about decided to leave when, like a flash mob, three people began to sing. After a couple of songs, the caroling ended.

The festivities were still going on; however, they decided it was time to head back to the parking area. As they left the yard of the homestead they remembered how pitch black it was and began giggling and teasing each other about staying on the path and not getting lost. Shari and Kelli were in the lead and were getting ahead of the other three. As they staggered through the darkness, Linda heard Shari say "Oh! My!" Linda asked if they were alright but didn't hear a reply. She began to get a little nervous. When Kara complained about her hands tingling, Jackie and Linda decided they might be holding her hands a little too tight! As they walked along staring into the night sky for any kind of light to see by, Linda felt a tug on her arm and heard a loud thump. A second later Kara said "MaMa just fell down". That is when the laughter began. Linda turned and felt around like Helen Keller. She found Jackie and Kara, on the ground laughing so hard they nearly wet themselves. When Linda realized Jackie had twisted her ankle and needed help, she yelled ahead to Shari and Kelli, "your momma is down!", "your Momma is down!", but they were too far ahead to hear so no help was coming. Linda and Kara helped Jackie up onto her one good foot and between the three of them, they finally made their way back to the car. They loaded into the car and headed home. When they arrived home, Kara jumped out of the car and began a blow-by-blow reenactment of their walk out of the homestead and back to the car in the pitch dark.

Linda and Jackie said they felt this newspaper article and their actual adventure taught Kara at the age of six and Kelli age three that you can't always believe what you read in the news and everyone sees and experiences things differently. It is still one of their most talked about and memorable adventures ever!

> "First the doctor told me the good news: I was going to have a disease named after me".
>
> Steve martin

Big Eddie…

I was asked if I had any stories about my brother, Jack Weldon, which most of you all will remember as Puncho. Our family had a serious thing about everyone having a nickname. For example, Gladys, Patricia, Terry, Jerry, and Jack were called Peg, Sissie, Boy, Smokey, and Puncho. Seems like they could remember Jack as easily as Puncho? Anyway, Puncho was around eight or nine when our mom passed away in 1954. Our dad had left and was living in California at the time. I believe it was a year or so that he came back and took Puncho back to California with him to live. I didn't see him for several years, until he was around sixteen or seventeen and could drive himself back. When he would return to Missouri it was always a grand gathering. Everyone would gather to see what sort of young man he was growing into. He was always the cool kid from California.

After he was married, he decided to move and bring his family back to Malden, Missouri. With him came one of his friends named "Big Eddie". Eddie was what we Missouri Hillbillies would call the typical Californian, he was around six feet two inches, 300 pounds, with a long ponytail kept up with a rubber band. Way cool dude!

Eddie was fascinated by our Missouri culture so, Puncho and I decided to show him the ropes. First, we took him to show him one of the rights of passage for the young men around the bootheel of Missouri, "Stealing watermelons". It was a well known fact that all watermelon growers donated the first few rows of melons to Missouri teenagers! NOT!!!

We also brought our wives who had never had this experience before. They would be the drivers for us, not that we needed to get away quickly, but you never knew when you might need to get back home, (in a hurry). We drove around just outside of Clarkton along a sandy ridge where the watermelons grew best until we found the perfect spot. Once we found it, we told the ladies to circle the block and pick us up in the very same place. Now, if you are from that are, you know the "blocks" are one mile square and it takes a while for someone who knew where they were going to get around, so two girls that had never been there before might take a little longer. And they were a little curious why we wanted them to drive with their headlights out until they got to the first turn and turn them off again when the rounded the last turn coming back. It was because we couldn't see the melons very well with the headlights in our eyes, yeah, that's it.

They were easing away while we briefed Big Eddie on how this system worked. We told him that it was very hard to tell the size of a watermelon while you were walking around in the patch, that it was much easier if you were crawling around, on your belly. Yeah, that's it.

Puncho and I could lay flatter that a spread-nanner (snake) if we had to, however, Big Eddie had a problem having a low profile. We crawled around a few minutes and all met back at the same spot as planned with two nice watermelons each. We sat up admiring each of our finds and looking for the girls when the first of many shotgun BBs rained down around us. I think we found the only farmer, that didn't have any watermelons to spare, and would like to have these six back. Puncho and I gave our four back immediately as we sprang to our feet and headed for the road ditch but Big Eddie wasn't about to give his up. That was fine with me; all I had to do was stay ahead of him. After the gunfire died down and we were all three lying in the road ditch wondering where the girls were with the car, Eddie decided that farmer was shooting at us. We told him it wasn't real bullets only salt rock he was shooting and it wouldn't sting very long. I also told Eddie, that the farmer couldn't shoot us after we made it to the road because the road wasn't his property, unless you were holding one of his watermelons! After the farmer reloaded and started shooting again, Puncho and I jumped into the car with the girls. We found Big Eddie down the road aways with one watermelon left.

The next week we took Big Eddie out "Stealing Pigeons".

> "I have six locks on my door all in a row. When I go out, I lock every other one. I figure no matter how long somebody stands there picking the locks, they are always locking three."
>
> elayne boosler

Bootheel Christmas…

I have many memories of growing up in the Bootheel of Missouri, but none quite as strong as Christmas morning. My Grandparents P.O. and Dollie Beasley raised me, however they had six or seven of their eleven children and some thirty other grandchildren also living within twenty five miles of our house. Of those Aunts and Uncles, I usually had my pick of where I wanted to spend Christmas Eve. As far back as I can remember, I was always welcome at any one of them and I think throughout the fifteen years I lived there, I spent Christmas Eve at each one of them.

It would be impossible to pick out the best one to write about, but there was one pretty memorable one. It was the "perfect" Christmas Eve with about six inches of fresh snow. I had decided to spend Christmas Eve at my Aunt Pauline and Uncle Ed's house just on the edge of Campbell, Missouri. They had four kids, Danny, Sue, Pam and Emily and lived in a single wide mobile home, barely room enough for their immediate family, but they always made room for me. My Aunt Pauline was like most women and she was very big on Christmas. She would always decorate their home and yard for the occasion. I'm not sure why that particular Christmas Eve, but my Granny and Grandpa decided to join us that year and that put nine people in this small trailer with the Christmas tree with lots of presents covering most of the living room floor. We were playing in what floor we could find when there was a knock at the door. Sue opened the door and there stood Uncle Leon and

Aunt Leona Beasley with their three kids, Jackie, Linda Carol and Ronald. Now there were fourteen of us. We were in the middle of our welcoming hugs when once again there was a knock at the door and there was Uncle Bill, Aunt Jean and cousin Debbie. Nice solid seventeen people in a trailer seemed to just about right.

My Aunts all lived within 15 miles of each other and talked to each other on the phone everyday that I can remember, my Uncle Cecil Kilgo would always said there are three ways to get the word out and they were; Telephone, Telegraph, and Tell-a-woman. No one could prove Uncle Cecil right better than Aunt Jean. As soon as she hit the door and could get to the phone she called the other Aunts that wasn't there. A rough estimate, but I would say Aunt Deaner and her six kids, Betty, Kathy, Fred, Rick, Jim and Tim showed up at the door about fifteen minutes later. Well, if it were possible to let the seams out on a mobile home, we sure needed it right about then.

The noise level was getting close to a small aircraft and the wallpaper was beginning to peel. The commode in the single bathroom began to flush and didn't stop for four hours. There were kids playing and an adult screaming at them in every room. Life was good!

As I left the bathroom and flushed the commode, I walked through one of the bedrooms I saw my Aunt Pauline showing off some dresses she had made for her girls right in front of the girls who were playing so hard they paid no attention to what she was saying. It was a clear case of hiding it right out in the open. I chuckled and moved on to the next bedroom where there were six boys between the ages of four and twelve playing "War". For those of you who saw the Normandy Beach scenes for the first ten minutes of "saving Private Ryan", well that is what that bedroom looked and sounded like. I only stood in the doorway for about ten seconds and I saw Rick and Dan die three time a piece. I had to move on quickly because that was my kind of room and I could feel myself getting sucked right into the battle. The next room was the kitchen where uncles Ed, Leon, and Bill sat talking about the Deer hunting experiences they had from just a few weeks before. Although I had slowly walked through that room, I really believe a great deal of that conversation was "mostly" true. I also remember they could hardly see each other for the cloud of cigarette smoke. Then I stepped into the living room where the TV was playing "It's a Wonderful Life" and Grandpa P.O. was sleeping on the couch like he was in a sound proof room. You know he was enjoying his knap by the slight stream of snuff running out of the right corner of his mouth and the faint scent of Colonel Lee whiskey. That is a smell you never forget. Looking back on the many Christmas Eves I spent in the Bootheel of Missouri that was one I will never forget. It turned into the perfect Christmas Eve.

"Never, under any circumstances, take a sleeping pill and a laxative on the same night."   Dave barry

Brothers...

I grew up in Southeast Missouri in the small town of Gideon. My grandparents raised me after my mother passed away of Multiple Sclerosis in 1954. When she first passed away, me, my sister, and my brother were taken in by our Grandpa and Granny Beasley. They had six children already gone from home and five still at home, adding three more mouths to feed was hard on them at best. I never heard one complaint about us being left with them and I stayed with them for fifteen years.

When mom passed away our dad lived in California. My brother Jack Weldon (Puncho) was about nine years old. After a few visits back home by dad, the decision was made for my brother to go live with him in California. I was too young to know what was happening back then.

I didn't see Puncho again for several years. I heard very little about how he was doing. I guess it is easier to adjust to whatever life you are dealt when you are young. The next time I can remember seeing my brother he was eighteen or nineteen years old. There were a few visits between those years but I don't remember the specifics. I can however remember that every visit was always met with great excitement each time he came "Home" by the entire family. I was always glad to see him and rekindle that brother's bond. No matter how long he was away from Southeast Missouri, it seemed as though he was constantly drawn back to his roots.

After Puncho married Chris Cunningham and they had a few children, Teresa, JoAnn, Holly, and Scott, he moved back to Malden to try to make a life for his new family. He was a painter by trade, like his dad, and was pretty much limited to that profession. It was hard to get started for him in Missouri and he soon had to return to California where he knew he could provide for his family. Although, I was starting my life out with a new bride, Colette, at the time, It was still hard to see him leave again. We never wrote each other in all of those years, but there was always a special bond that I can't explain. I do know why I was always very excited to see him when he came to visit.

Puncho was the restless sort, to say the least. He had a hard time staying in one place for an extended period of time. He lived all over Southern California, Utah, Arizona and probably some places I missed. He lived in Mesa Arizona when my family and I returned from being stationed in Lakenheath, England in 1977. We went on leave and drove down there from Las Vegas where we were stationed at the time. We camped on the Verde river with him and his family in the Arizona desert. It was a great four day weekend. One I will always remember. We were all returning from a swim in the river when we discovered a small rattlesnake in our path. Puncho killed it and later skinned it and made a hat ban for my hat. I never wore that hat again!

While we were stationed at Eglin AFB, in Ft Walton, Florida in 1983 Puncho came down to visit. We convinced him to move down to Ft Walton so we could spend some time together. He could always swing a deal and this time was no different. He found a small house and traded with the landlord to paint it for a few months free rent. In a few days he had it looking like a doll house as he always could. There was some issues with his wife and they never moved down. He returned to St Louis and our lives went on.

When I retired from the Air Force in 1994, we were living in Navarre, Florida. I started a Handyman business and had three or four paper routes to supplement my retirement. Puncho came through on his way to visit our sister Pat, (Sissie) who lived in Okeechobee, Florida at the time. I talked him into coming in with me and adding his painting expertise to my handyman business. He agreed and within a few days we had an agreement with Century 21 Realty to paint their rental property between tenants. We were beginning to get on our feet and Puncho got a case of "Restless Leg Syndrome". It was again time for him to move on. I wasn't very happy about that, but as a brother, I understood and continued with my life.

Later that summer went down to Okeechobee to visit my sister and he was already living in a nice little house right on Lake Okeechobee. He was in heaven. Working at what he loved best and fishing every day. I began going down and fishing with him two or three times a year. Those were great trips and we both enjoyed them. I couldn't imagine him living anywhere else; until my sister moved back to Malden, Missouri. I'm not sure how long he remained there after Sis moved, but it didn't seem very long until he was moving to Ohio. I knew his health was deteriorating and his ability to paint was becoming limited. I hated to see him leave the lake and that great South Florida weather, besides the fact that he was putting a serious dent in my free fishing trips!

He lasted about six months in Ohio before packing it in and moving back to Missouri. I now live in Ohio and I honestly understand why he didn't stay here long. It is too cold up here. Puncho returned to Missouri, found him a little place to rent and adjusted to living on a fixed income of Social

Security and the odd painting job. We try to attend our family reunion every year where we get to visit for four or five days with each other. We talk on the phone usually weekly or more.

Recently he has moved to Clarkton, Missouri where he is house sitting in my Uncle Ed's house until my cousin Danny Beasley will retire and move back home. It is a good opportunity for Puncho and wonderful gesture from "The Beasley Kids". I appreciate it and I know Puncho does too. Thanks to my Uncle Smokey, Puncho still gets a chance to fish pretty often by joining him and Aunt Georgia at their campsite at various lakes in and around their local area. Although we were never really geographically close, we have had a special bond that I guess only brothers can have. I know that I am sixty four now and he is around sixty nine and I am still just as excited to see him as I was when I was fifteen. 17 Aug 2014 we lost my brother. He went fishing with the Lord. Can't explain it, but there is just something special about "brotherly Love"…

Cleat Monsters…

I grew up living a half mile out of town of Gideon, Missouri, which generally never bothered me. It was a small country town where nothing much ever happened. There was definitely nothing supernatural there. Even when I was very young I would walk to school and back and never thought a thing about it. It was about a half mile out of town with nothing on either side of the road but cotton fields. On the way to school, there were four or five school buses that passed my house every morning. I could have stepped out on the porch and any one of them would have stopped and picked me up for school. Most mornings I would go ahead and walk, or if I did ride the bus, it was generally Vernon Tolbert's bus. Vernon always looked out for me and he had the best looking daughters in the county! In the afternoon there was always someone walking from the school to the ballpark across the road from my house that I could walk with.

Also, living in a small town like Gideon, it was pretty hard to walk anywhere because you knew everyone and everyone knew you, so as soon as you hit the road, someone stopped to pick you up. I remember hitch-hiking from Gideon, all the way to Malden, (10 miles) to sell Grit newspapers, visit cousins, or see a movie without fear of being abducted, or molested. Unfortunately, that is no longer the case. You can't even let your kids play in the yard these days. It is a shame that today's children are missing a fantastic part of their lives, but it isn't their fault.

When I got old enough I started playing baseball. If the game was being played across the road from our house, I simply got ready and walked across the road. After the game I would walk with several people on their way back into town and stop off at our house. Because the coach would sometimes drag the field after the game, I would be at home and in bed before the ballpark lights were turned out.

If the games were "away" games, I would walk to school and catch the bus with everyone else going to the game. I would get busy talking with my friends on the way back home, I would remain on the bus as it passed my home and ride on into town, causing me to have to walk back home in the dark, alone.

Gideon was a small town, but it did have street lights until you reached three ditch bridge heading East from town, as you crossed the bridge the street lights were non-existent. From that bridge it was a little over a quarter-mile to our house and it was darker than dark! If it was a full moon I could see just fine, however, when there was no moon, the only way I knew I was heading down the road correctly was when an on-coming car's headlights shined on the white lines for ten seconds.

Now for some reason, as I remember, there never was a

moon out when we had an away game. Which means when I had to walk over three ditch bridge into the darkness, I could hear them, the cleat monsters! I could never see them, but I knew they were right there on my heels, breathing down the back of my neck. They were extremely fast, a car could come by and I would stop quickly, turn to look, and they were no where to be seen. After the car had passed and I began walking again, there they were, right behind me again. I would speed up to a trot and so would they, if I weaved across the road left to right, so did they. The strangest things about the cleat monsters was when I crossed the railroad tie we had across the road ditch in front of the house, they were gone. The strangest thing about those cleat monsters and the only thing I could ever figure out was that they must have been afraid of our house or something, because I never heard them in our yard.

"If you think nobody cares if you're alive, try missing a couple of car payments."

flip Wilson

Cotton Sacks…

For those of you that never had the "pleasure" of picking cotton, you have missed a piece of Americana that few have "enjoyed". The cotton sack started out as a cotton basket I believe. Later they began using burlap sack, then, moved on to the better known cotton sack made of canvas. The standard cotton sack when I was dragging one was a seven foot sack and a nine foot sack. They had wide shoulder straps to prevent the canvas from cutting into your shoulder as the sack was filled with cotton. When the sack became to "wear in" the strap would begin to roll and cut against your shoulder anyway, not that I ever had enough cotton in my sack to cause much pain. The men that picked cotton as their main income back then would use their feet to pack the cotton into the sack.

Back then they paid three cents per pound or $3.00 per one hundred pounds of cotton and they wanted to "weight in" with one hundred pounds of cotton in their sack each time. I focused on one hundred pounds per day. I think my Granny Beasley cooked three meals per day and still picked 150 pounds of cotton. My Uncles Edd and Leon would pick 400-500 pounds per day and their wives would pick 200 pounds, so they would make $18.00 - $20.00 per day back in the early 1960s.

It was back breaking work. In the early 1960s the cotton wasn't very tall, so you would have to bend over to pick the cotton off of the stalk. This would really hurt you back after a while. To ease the pain, you would get on your knees to straighten your back while you picked for a while, however, this caused your knees to hurt so, it was back on your feet and bend over again. This went on all day. Some folks bought wool lined leather knee pads. I could never keep the darn things on my legs. They kept falling down around my ankles when I stood up and they hurt the back of my legs when I was down on my knees. Just wearing those things was an art in itself.

It is hard to explain how to pick cotton, but the shape of the cotton boll once opened fit the human hand perfectly. When the bolls are mature, they opened to reveal the white cotton inside. There were four or five pieces of cotton inside the boll called squares and oddly enough, most of us had five fingers. You simply reached in between the hulls and "picked" the cotton square out and placed it in the cotton sack. You would pick as many squares as you could hold in your hands before placing it in the cotton sack. Sounds pretty simple, however, the hull had a nice pointed tip that would consistently find it's way underneath your cuticles or just stick right into your finger tip. After a while your hands were as tender as a young mother's love! Because you are working with cotton, your hands will get dry and the cotton will not release from the hull very easy. That's when "Cotton Picker's Friend" came out. This stuff appears to be made of some sort of clear mucus with a touch of glue in it. It's purpose is to help the cotton stick to your fingertips and a side effect was to burn your cuts and scratches until you want to cry. Believe me it did it's job when it came to the side effect! There was nothing friendly about Cotton Picker's Friend!

As I said they paid you by the pound and the most money was made very early in the morning when the dew was heavy on the cotton. Wet cotton weighed more than dry cotton. I remember they would "knock off" weight if you were picking cotton in the dew. Also dirt would help your cotton weigh a little more, so if a small dirt clod were to get mixed in with your cotton, well, sometimes it just happened. That is why the Field straw boss would be the one that weigh the cotton and watch out to make sure you had "clean" cotton with no trash or dirt in it.

The first mechanical pickers were only capable of harvesting one row of cotton at a time, but were still able to replace up to forty hand laborers. The current cotton picker is a self-propelled machine that removes cotton lint and seed (seed-cotton) from the plant at up to six rows at a time. The other type of picker is the "spindle" picker. It uses rows of barbed spindles that rotate at high speed and remove the seed-cotton from the plant. The seed-cotton is then removed from the spindles by a counter-rotating doffer and is then blown up into the basket. Once the basket is full the picker dumps the seed-cotton into a "module builder". The module builder creates a compact "brick" of seed-cotton, weighing in at approximately 21,000 lb (16 un-ginned bales), which can be stored in the field or in the "gin yard" until it is ginned. Each ginned bale weighs roughly 480 lb (218.2 kg).

When all of the picking was done by hand, my grandpa was the Straw boss and he would drive the tractor pulling the trailer full of cotton to the gin. When I was young and the trailer was full at the end of the day I would get to ride in the cotton to the gin. Laying back in the cotton as we crawled down the road was a memory you won't forget. The orange sunsets, the sounds of the old "popping Johnny" tractor and the smells of the cotton, were actually soothing in some odd way. I guess if you asked any one that has had that experience, they would tell you the same thing. It was hard and tiring work, but it would make you appreciate every penny you made.

I can still flash back to that time. It is like your Grandma's kitchen in the summer time, something you will never forget. Go ahead, take yourself back there every once in a while, you'll feel better for it…

Growing up in Missouri…

1. You've never met any celebrities.
2. Everyone you know has been on a "Float Trip,"
3. "Vacation" means driving to Silver Dollar City, Worlds of Fun or Six Flags.
4. You've seen all the biggest bands ten years AFTER they were popular.
5. You measure distance in minutes rather than miles. For example, "Well, Hannibal is only 40 minutes away."
6. Down south to you means Springfield or Branson.
7. The phrase "I'm going to the Lake this weekend" only means one thing.
8. You know several people who have hit a deer.
9. You think Missouri is spelled with an "ah" at the end.
10. Your school classes were canceled because of cold.
11. You know what "Party Cove" is.
12. Your school classes were canceled because of heat.
13. You instinctively ask someone you've just met, "What High School did you go to?"
14. You've had to switch from "heat" to "A/C" in the same day.
15. You think ethanol makes your truck "run a lot better."
16. You know what's knee-high by the Fourth of July.
17. You see people wear bib overalls at funerals.
18. You see a car running in the parking lot at the store with no one in it, no matter what time of day.
19. You know in your heart that Mizzou can beat Nebraska in football.

20. You end your sentences with an unnecessary preposition. Example: "Where's my coat at?"
21. All the festivals across the state are named after a fruit, vegetable, season or grain.
22. You install security lights on your house and garage and leave both unlocked.
23. You think of the major four food groups as beef, pork, beer, and Jell-O salad with marshmallows.
24. You carry jumper cables in your car and know that everyone else should.
25. You went to skating parties as a kid.
26. You only own three spices: salt, pepper, and ketchup.
27. You design your kid's Halloween costume to fit over a snowsuit.
28. You think sexy lingerie is tube socks and a flannel nightie.
29. The local paper covers national and international headlines on one page, but requires six pages for sports.
30. You think I-44 is spelled and pronounced "farty-far." (St. Louis only.)
31. You'll pay for your kids to go to college unless they want to go to KU.
32. You think that "deer season" is a National Holiday.
33. You know that Concordia is halfway between Kansas City and Columbia, and Columbia is halfway between St. Louis and Kansas City, and the Warrenton Outlet Mall is halfway between Columbia and St. Louis.
34. You can't think of anything better than sitting on the porch in the middle of the summer during a thunderstorm.

35. You know which leaves make good toilet paper.
36. You've said, "It's not the heat, it's the humidity."
37. You know all four seasons: Almost Summer, Summer, Still Summer and Football.
38. You know if another Missourian is from the Bootheel, Ozarks, Eastern, Middle or Western Missouri soon as they open their mouth.
39. You know that Harry S Truman, Walt Disney and Mark Twain are all from Missouri.
40. You failed World Geography in school because you thought Cuba, Versailles, California, Nevada, Houston, Cabool, Louisiana, Springfield, and Mexico were cities in Missouri. (And they are!) (Additionally, so are Memphis, Cairo, and Florida)
41. You think a traffic jam is ten cars waiting to pass a tractor.
42. You know what "HOME OF THE THROWED ROLL" means.
43. You actually get this and forward it to all your Missouri friends.

Author Unknown -

Cotton Picken' Vacation…

In the Bootheel of Missouri during the 1960s the Summer school break was called Cotton Vacation. The best I remember about vacations, they were for taking your family somewhere and enjoying something you didn't do during the rest of the year. If that is the true definition, then I guess Cotton Vacation would fall into that category, because that is something I did not do during the rest of the year!

Around 1961 I was eleven years old and kept telling my Grandpa and Hershel Bell, the farm's owner that I was ready to drive a tractor and get away from the cotton hoe and the cotton sack. It took about a week of cotton vacation to convince them that I was right. They gave me a chance at driving a tractor. First they put me on a small Ford Ferguson tractor, pulling a harrow, which we pronounced "har". No sense wasting your breathe on two syllables when one would do the trick. The har was made of 8 foot iron beams with railroad spikes welded to them. With the weight of the iron and the tip of the spike pointing down it wasused to break up the gumbo clods. This was done on the field before it is planted so they guessed I couldn't do much damage with it. I was out in the wide open field in the middle of the day. One of those days were the dirt was almost too hot to walk on. From the highway I suppose I looked like Charlie Brown's friend, Pig-Pen with the cloud of dust around me all day. Speaking of dust, do you remember being out in the cotton patch, or beans, or corn and every dust devil that came through managed to hit you? Why was that? Anyway, I was driving along pulling the har and watching the other tractor in the next field turn at the end row without slowing down. I figured I had been driving a tractor for two days now, I was pretty much the best around. At first I would slow down at the end of the field and turn without braking. That went pretty well so the next time I slowed a little less until eventually I could spin the steering wheel and BAM! There I was heading back the other way. The problem was I wasn't lined up nice and straight after I made the turn so the pattern I was leaving wasn't quite feng-shui, (Fung-Shway) and that was bad ju-ju! I mulled on it a while and on my return trip I saw my Grandpa and the Hershel Bell setting in the truck at the end of the field watching me. I figured it was time to show my stuff so at the end of the field I made a hard left turn and added some left brake with it. This made the tractor turn almost on a dime, but because I was dragging the har it didn't swing out and away from the tractor like it had been doing, instead it began climbing up the left rear tractor tire and after me!. I managed to hit the brakes before the spikes made it to me. They told me to shut off the tractor, get down and go with them. I was fired on the spot!

After begging for another few days I talked them into letting me back on the tractor. This time they gave me the same little Ford Ferguson and instead of a harrow, it had a small disk on it. Guess they thought I couldn't get this one climbing the rear tires. My job with the disk was to disk all of the fence rows to keep the weeds from spreading to the crops. I understood that and off I went. I never realized every field had four sides and that meant lots of weeds. I was back near the railroad tracks, near the three ditch trussle, one day disking right against the fence. I was going pretty slow to make sure I got as close to the fence as I could. I noticed the Mr Bell's truck drive up to the fence at the end of the field I was in and stopped. I wasn't worried because I was going very slow and in a straight line. If you've ever driven a tractor before you will notice that they have an automatic "wedgie" inserter built right in the seat. About one hundred yards from the truck I stood up on the tractor to remove this giant wedgie. When my knee hit the throttle causing the tractor to lung forward, causing me to fall back down in the seat, causing my knee to hit the throttle again slowing the tractor down. When I managed to get the throttle under control, without my knowledge, I had turned the wheel into the fence, fearing I was too close, I snapped it back causing the disk to swing out and grab the fence behind me. I had dragged about twenty feet of fence down the road before I could get the tractor stopped. They told me to shut off the tractor, get down and go with them. I was fired again!

After about a week of doing nothing but sharpening plow tips, I got a reprieve and was allowed to get back on the tractor. This time it was on a John Deere and using a rear end cultivator. They must have been really short-handed that summer. Now this was a little tricky because I thought you had to look backwards to see the plows and forward to keep the tractor straight. They did explain this operation a little more than the others. The Hershel Bell and my Grandpa both also explained all about the value of a cotton plant and how important it was NOT to plow up. I went extremely slow until I figured this one out. Then I began to speed up as I got more comfortable with it. Pretty soon I was keeping up with the other tractors in the field. After a couple of days of this I could not move my neck at all and my shoulders and arms were so tense and I began to look like a twelve year old senior citizen when I got off of the tractor. At the beginning of the week I was jumping down from the tractor at the end of the day and running into the house. By the end of week, I was making sure I hit every step coming off that thing, and parking closer to the back door! We were almost finished plowing for the first round and I had to go back to school soon. I was plowing my last Friday afternoon, feeling good about my accomplishments that summer. No cotton sacks all summer and I was proud of that. I was plowing in a field that had a field road about three feet higher than the crop growing on it to keep the water off of it I guess. I saw Hershel's truck stop on the field road where I was about to come out to. I wasn't worried because I had done very well for the past few days. They were all smiles and waving at me. When I reached the end of the row, raised the plows, spun the tractor around, dropped the plows and headed back to the other end. It went flawless! After a few seconds of feeling good about myself, I had to turn to see what they thought of my feat. When I turned, I saw them both out of the truck running after me. Apparently when I turned at the end of the row, I caught the outer plow tip on the bank of the field road causing it to turn inward and now it was plowing down the center of the cotton row. I had plowed up about one hundred feet of cotton before I stopped. They told me to shut off the tractor, get down and go with them.... My Vacation was over!

> How is it one careless match can start a forest fire, but it takes a whole box to start a campfire?
>
> anonymous

Cousins…

When I was growing up, I had thirty eight first cousins living within fifty miles of our house. We all thought "Fun" was our middle names. This year we will have our thirty sixth family reunion and I will see most of them there. It is still just as exciting as it was thirty five years ago. If you include "Cousin-in-laws", if there is such a thing, you can add another fifty.

My cousins were my first and best friends. They love me for who I am. They taught me about life. Literally! My cousin Wayman was the first person to explain to me the "birds and the bees." After I heard his story, I went to his sisters, Carmel and Carolyn and told them someone needs to have the "Sex" talk with that boy!

My brother, sister and I were orphaned when I was four years old and our Grandparents took us in even with seven children already gone from home and four still at home. That gave me eleven Aunts and Uncles producing thirty eight first cousins to fill my life and provide my family values until I met my wife, Colette.

Now I'm not saying my cousins were the "perfect" role models. Some of the things they taught me, intentionally or not, were perhaps borderline illegal and when it came to the male cousins, most of the time immoral. That was what I thought was so cool about them. I always had my Granny and Grandpa to help me decide which of my cousin's "life-lessons" I should listen to or ignore!

The male cousins taught me things like, men don't cry, how to bait a fish hook, and most of all, how to properly turn over an outhouse at Halloween. These were valued lessons that I have never forgotten. The female cousins on the other hand, taught me the how to understand the female species. Need I say they weren't very good in structors. I still don't understand women. One thing they taught me was if you laugh too hard, you will pee your pants. I have been very careful with that lesson, most of the time!

I remember when the family would all gather at our house on Sunday, which was often, there would be cousins everywhere. Every time the day would start out boys and girls separate, but by the middle of the afternoon it was a free for all. The best part about it was no matter where I went, whether it was in the house, barn, or yard there was someone I enjoyed being around.

They taught me how to stand up for myself, how to laugh when I would rather have cried, and how to entertain myself when necessary. They gave me skills that I would use for the rest of my life.

I have cousins who are twelve years older than me and cousins who are twelve years younger than me. However, the great part about us is, when we are all together we are all the same age.

I joined the Air Force and raised my children as Air Force brats moving all over the world. We tried to return home every year to our family reunion so they can meet and stay in touch with their cousins, it always made me sad that they never got to experience cousins like I did. It is good to see that my kids are trying to let their kids stay in touch with their cousins. I enjoy watching my grandkids becoming pals with each other as they grow up.

Though most of us are now separated by distance, I am more than thankful for a wonderful childhood because of my cousins.

So, if you stop by the B & B reunion at Sam A. Baker Park in Southeast Missouri every fourth of July, you will see lots of cousins having lots of fun. Just be sure and bring an extra pair of underwear because there will be some serious laughing…

"Children: You spend the first 2 years of their life teaching them to walk and talk. Then you spend the next 16 telling them to sit down and shut-up".

anonymous

Davis Groceries…

I grew up living a half mile out of town of Gideon, Missouri in the same house from 1953 to 1968. I was three years old when we moved in and eighteen years old when I moved out. Looking back, it was a large part what made me who I am today. My family values were shown to me by example, not only by my grandparents, but by most everyone I came in contact with growing up in Gideon.

One of those people was H.E. Davis, "Homer" I think, the owner of a small grocery store in town. I think his trademark was his white butcher's apron. I never saw him without it on. Mr Davis had to have known every kid in town by name and those he didn't know, his wife Georgia, did.

Mr Davis always had a soft voice and a soft smile when you walked into his store. Georgia, however seemed to be a little on the "Grumpy" side. She also seemed to know a lot about everyone in town, but I guess if every woman in town stopped by and had a chit-chat with her, them she couldn't help but know all about everyone. They also had a daughter, Hazel that worked at the store. She was more like her dad, sort of quite.

I worked for Mr Davis a few times sweeping the store and the sidewalk out in front of the store. I don't really think he needed the help, but, was just giving me a little spending money.

Because there were limited places to eat during our school lunch period, some of us would hurry down to Davis Groceries and have a bologna or ham sandwich and a sodie for lunch. Mr Davis would fix it just like you wanted it and he used that fresh, soft Wonder Bread. I can smell it right now. I liked my bologna about a half inch thick with cheese and mustard on it. We would get our sodie and sandwich and go over on the side of the store where the burlap sacks were stacked. They were filled with taters, flour, beans and such. We would sit on the sacks and enjoy our sandwiches and cool drinks.

Mr Davis would fix your sandwich first then, if you didn't have the money to pay for it, he just put it on your parent's bill. Fifteen cents for a sandwich and ten cents for a sodie.

I remember one day in late December, 1962 me and a half dozen other kids were sitting around the coal stove enjoying our sandwiches listening over the half wall that divided the store, to Mrs Davis talk about someone's hardship just loud enough for us to hear. The weather was getting bad with some sleet mixed with snow coming down on top of what had already fell yesterday and partially melted then refrozen. The coal stove sure felt good after our brisk walk from the school. I sure was glad I had on my coat and warm boots. I hate it when my feet are cold. That day I remember seeing three kids come in to the store with lightweight coats on with torn sleeves at the shoulders. Their shoes were definitely wrong for the season. They were new to Gideon I was sure because, like Mr and Mrs Davis, I knew almost everyone in town. I thought they had came in to get some sandwiches for lunch, but as they huddled around the stove to warm their hands and feet, I could quickly see they had no money to buy the 15 cent sandwich. I overheard Mrs Davis say to Mr Davis something about kids just making themselves at home in a place of business. Mr Davis went to the rear of the store, stirred around for a couple of minutes and returned with three sandwiches and three chocolate sodies. He smiled as he gave them to the three children and never said a word. We were all silent for a few minutes thinking about what had just happened. Even though I was a 12 year old boy, I was mighty proud to know a man like Mr Davis and hoped I would be like him some day. I think without realizing it, Mr Davis had taught me a valuable lesson and I am sure the other six kids sitting around that stove that day lucky enough to be able to buy our lunch, felt the same way.

Mrs Davis had her receipt book and a pencil ready to document the lunches when Mr Davis returned to the counter. Mr Davis took the book and the pencil from her hands and laid them back on the counter. Nothing was written anywhere.

Although I will never live up to Mr Davis' standards no matter how hard I try, one of the things I did learn from him was, "If you have it, share it"... Thanks Mr Davis for setting the example.

"Nothing sucks more than that moment during an argument when you realize you're wrong."   anonymous

Ann's Patch…

As I have mentioned before in another story, we lived as sharecroppers for a gentleman named Hershel Bell. He was very good to our family and cared for all of the children. My Aunt Ann Beasley was one of the oldest girls in our household and Hershel really liked her. Wanting to do something to help Ann, one summer before her senior year in high school he came to her to make a deal with her. He proposed that if she would take care of the three acre plot in the corner of his farmland that he would let her have the profits from that three acres and take care of her senior year. This meant she could pay for her senior ring, all the clothes she needed and finance her "Senior Trip" to Daytona Beach at the end of the year. Ann was so excited about this agreement she began tending to the land before they even planted there.

When it was time to plant and plow, she was right there taking excellent care of those three acres. Unfortunately, Ann was killed in a car accident before she could enjoy the profits from that little patch of ground. From that time forward, that little three acres was affectionately known as "Ann's Patch".

"I dream of a better tomorrow, where chickens can cross the road and not be questioned about their motives."

anonymous

Dirt under your fingernails...

Growing up on a small farm in the 1960s was full of activities. There was no "sleeping in". You were up early, you ate breakfast every morning and you were outside. I don't ever remember turning on the TV when I got up in the morning unless it was a school day and I would watch Captain Kangaroo before I caught the bus to school. The Summer days were spent riding your bike, playing war or some sort of sport. My favorite sport was batting rocks across the road. I still believe it should be a Olympic event! I was too short to really enjoy basketball, but when my Grandpa used one of those cable spools for a backstop, I thought I was "Up Town". Most of the time I still just had a rim with no net.

The farm was great for exploring. There must have been a thousand different types of bugs on the farm, and I can proudly say I have roasted almost all of them. We were pretty much free to go where we wanted to, we also knew there were some dangerous placing on the farm, especially around the farming equipment, yet, like most kids, we sometimes ignored those hazards and created a few scars from it.

We weren't expected to work in the fields when we were young, but we were expected to start our training by working in the flower and vegetable gardens, both of which were usually overseen by "Mom" or "Granny" and that wasn't always a cakewalk!

Taking Responsibility was a natural lesson that came with farm life. If you used it and you broke it, then you fixed it. When something needed to be done, you simply did it to the best of your ability. No one would fault you for trying, but everyone would get after you for not trying. Looking back I had a lot of fun and gained valuable skills that have continued to help me in my adult life. I also credit these experiences with allowing me to meet new people and giving me a chance to do develop my social skills. I did not grow up in an era where you were told "don't speak to strangers". That is exactly how you got to know people. It was how we learned who to trust and not to trust.

Farm life did not allow for "vacation time", at least not in the way that urban families take vacations. Most farmers took short trips to go camping or visit with relatives. A vacation for me was at least one night away from the farm. I had cousins that lived in South St Louis that I would spend time with in the Summer. That was very different from farm life. Growing up on a farm and being involved in farm activities allowed me to understand plant, human and animal relationships, develop a sense of responsibility and gain skills and experiences that have helped me even if though I did not choose become a farmer. If you paid attention to the markets for cotton, corn, wheat, etc., you would have gained valuable knowledge of how the system works in the United States.

The first supermarket supposedly appeared on the American landscape around 1946. That is not very long ago. Until then, where was all the food? Well folks, the food was in homes, gardens, local fields. It was near kitchens and on tables. It was in the pantry, the cellar, the backyard.

I grew up on a farm. I left home and joined the military. After 20 years, I retired from the U.S. Air Force and now work on computer systems known as Flight Simulators used to train USAF pilots to fly military aircraft. This is about as far away from farming as you can get, however, my heart still holds a warm spot for the farm. Sometimes I miss the dirt under my fingernails…

Here is a quote that pretty much sums it up for me:

"Why do farmers farm, given their economic adversities on top of the many frustrations and difficulties normal to farming? And always the answer is: "Love. They must do it for love." Farmers farm for the love of farming. They love to watch and nurture the growth of plants. They love to live in the presence of animals. They love to work outdoors. They love the weather, maybe even when it is making them miserable. They love to live where they work and to work where they live. If the scale of their farming is small enough, they love to work in the company of their children and with the help of their children. They love the measure of independence that farm life can still provide. I have an idea that a lot of farmers have gone to a lot of trouble merely to be self-employed to live at least a part of their lives without a boss."

---Wendell Berry, Bringing it to the Table: Writings on Farming and Food

"By working faithfully eight hours a day you may eventually get to be boss and work twelve hours a day".   robert frost

Dust Devils…

I was raised just outside of the town of Gideon, Missouri, just across the road from the baseball field. A field that looks like a, "Build it, and they will come" sorta field, use to be a cotton patch or a corn field I'm sure. I lived there from age four to the beginning of my senior year in high school when my Grandpa P.O. Beasley retired from farming and bought a house in Clarkton, Missouri, my greatest rival! Thanks to Vernon Tolbert for re-routing the school bus to pick me up and Dennis Skidmore for coming after me in the mornings, I was able to finish my senior year at Gideon, Thanks again Vernon and Dennis.

I was driving home from work yesterday here at Wright-Patterson AFB, Ohio, which felt like the first day without snow during my first year here, when I spotted a farmer disking his field preparing for a corn crop. It was a warm day with a gentle breeze and he looked like Charlie Brown's friend, Pig-Pen with a ball of dust all around him. This took me back to the fields between three ditch and four ditch just East of Gideon where we worked on Hershel Bell's farm. I remembered chopping soybeans and it was 95 degrees with 75 percent humidity and the gumbo was like a powder somewhere around 100 plus degrees on my bare feet. We would go as long as we could and we had to stop and bury our feet underneath the hot layer of dust to where it was cooler, or in the shade of some bean stalks.

Leaning on my hoe while my feet cooled, wishing it would rain out of the single cloud in the sky, so that we might get to go to the house early. I felt a nice breeze start up and was ready for a few minutes of cooling for the rest of my body. Within seconds I was in the middle of a dust devil as it filled my eyes with that powered gumbo. It was gone as quickly as it came. I could see it twirling its way towards everyone in the field. Some bonnets were blown off the women's heads and the men had to hold on to their caps to keep them from blowing away. Sometimes there would be several dust devils in an hour dancing across those fields. We don't know what starts them and we don't know what stops them, we just randomly see them all over the fields. Another place that seemed to draw these dust devils was the baseball field. It was like a magnet for them. I often wondered what lured them to the ballgames.

You can see in the picture below where a dust devil is hitting yet another baseball game, but the other photo is a dust devil on the planet Mars. I guess you can run, but you can't hide from the dust devil.

Fences…

Growing up on a small farm just East of Gideon, Missouri, we had fences only to keep the livestock and the poultry in their pens. There was no such thing as a fenced in yard. Why on earth would you fence in a yard? Just didn't make much sense. We had nothing to keep in or out of our yard. There were times when men would pull into our driveway, park their car or truck out in the corner of the yard, and go hunting in the fields out back of our house. We respected their vehicles and they respected our property. It was as simple as that.

There were those who lived in town that wanted to have a cute little picket fence to decorate their yard. It also identified their property lines when they built their house too close to someone else. These fences were mostly for decoration and came in all shapes and sizes.

Through the years as kids got a little more mischievous some people had to build fences for their back yards a little higher and a little stronger to try and hang on to what little material things they had. Storage sheds with locks began showing up in most back yards.

As the sexual revolution began to allow a lot less clothing out in public, and sun bathing became a popular thing to do, clothing in the back yard was even less. This is where privacy fences came into play, allowing the female species the ability to tan every inch of skin they could legally get away with. I never have figured that out, "Why tan it, if you weren't going to show it off to someone"?

While we were trying to protect our property and our ladies, we were unintentionally isolating ourselves from each other. The privacy fence not only blocked the thieves and peeping toms, it also blocked our basic form of socializing, simply talking to our neighbor.

We have in some cases went from, "That sweet old couple that sat in their yard and waved at every passerby", do you remember them?, to "That weird old couple with the electric privacy fence all around their property and the pit bulls in their yard. Do you know them?.

Now I am not talking about everyone out there. However, there have been enough fence builders over the years to impact our society. There are hundreds of thousands in America that have lived next to their neighbor for five or more years and can't even tell you their names. I believe fences have been a major factor in this relationship.

Free Go Cart…

One of the weekends I was spending at Uncle Edd's comes back to me often. Around nine o'clock one Saturday morning Dan and I were stirring around in the back yard looking for something to tinker with, we were going through the junk pile, which was more like a vein of gold to a couple of 12 year old boys when we ran upon a Briggs and Stratton engine. We both spotted this gem at the same time, turned and looked each other in the eyes with the exact same thought running through our head; we are positive we could have us a go cart running by supper. It was going to be a classic two seater. I would handle the steering wheel and Dan would man the hand brake and we didn't need no stinking roll bars!

Before this masterpiece could come to life, we had to get the Briggs running. Because we were already master mechanics at twelve years old, that shouldn't be a problem. We took the engine out of the junk pile and hurried to the "pit" to get it going. The pit at that time was a fifty-five gallon barrel with a couple of two by fours laid across it. It was the ideal work bench, we could reach everything on top of the engine and the crankshaft hung down into the barrel out of the way. Perfectly stable.

Of course there was no cover on the engine and the flywheel was open to the elements on top. With no cover on it, that meant there was no starter rope, just a groove where the rope went. This was not a problem for us, we simply found us a three foot section of clothesline and we were off to the races, so to speak. I wrapped the clothesline cord around the groove on top of the engine a couple of times while my pit crew, (Dan), held fast to the engine block. I gave it a good firm jerk on the cord and we both almost pissed our pants, the cotton picking thing started! As we were dancing around like a couple of school girls, we noticed the engine was vibrating around the top of the two by fours and was about to slip off and down into the barrel. I ran over to the barrel as the engine was slipping off the board and heading down. I couldn't let that happen, so I reached down into the barrel and grabbed the top of the engine by the flywheel… did I mention the engine was running and there was no cover on it! Yes, I actually did grab that engine by the "spinning" flywheel. Needless to say, I let go faster than I grabbed it.

We both stood there a second wondering what had happened and what to do next when Dan said "is that blood on your hand"? Looking down at the thumb on my left hand, I won't lie to you, I nearly fainted. The left half of the nail was curled back from the cuticle to the tip of the thumb and I could clearly see my heartbeat!

Being the cool guy that I am, I looked at Dan and said, "does that look right to you"? Because it was numb, we could sort of chuckle about it until the blood flow became more of a spurt than a drip.

All of the women were gone somewhere and Uncle Edd was asleep after working midnight shift. We walked into his bedroom, dreading to have to wake him up, but knowing this was not good, Dan nudged him and as he was trying to wake and come to his senses, I stuck, what now was looking more like a young squash than a thumb right up in his face, blood pouring everywhere. He jumped like it was the mafia tossing a horse head in bed with him. Being cool like I was, I said, "should we do something about this"? Then to be honest, the rest of that day is a blur…

"America is a country where half the money is spent buying food, the other half is spent trying to lose weight".

anonymous

Girls…

I started to school at Gideon elementary school in Gideon, Missouri in 1956. It was a whole new world compared to the small farm house I had been in most of my life. The first thing I noticed, even at the age of six was the girls! They were everywhere and they were different. They wore frilly little dresses so they couldn't wrestle good. They had little bows in their hair so their hair wouldn't get in their eyes. You could say something harmless like "stupid ole girl", and they would start crying. At age six they really weren't much fun.

I think it was after "Cotton vacation" when I turned twelve I began to adjust my perspective on girls. They weren't quite as dumb as I had previously thought and I was beginning to see things in those dresses that I had not noticed before. I think I had changed my whole idea about wrestling with them that summer also. But, they still cried at the drop of a hat. That still had me baffled.

Finally at the beginning of the 1963 school year I decided it was time to start trying to talk to girls. That was a little tough for me. They knew nothing about the New York Yankees or the St Louis Cardinals. They couldn't put a worm on a hook or catch grasshoppers for bait. I knew exactly what you can do with boys, but I just couldn't quite figure out what to do with girls. They walked funny and they smelled funny. But one thing I did notice was they were getting thriftier because those dresses they wore were getting smaller. I thought that was a good idea, just didn't know why I thought that.

1966 I got my driver's license and I was still confused on the purpose of girls. Were they there just to spend money on? When I went to the movies with my buds, I didn't have to pay for them to get in and buy them popcorn and sodies. Now I wasn't a complete idiot. I knew how to hold hands and how to sneak my arm around one at the movies. I went home many times with no blood circulation in my left arm for thirty minutes because I had my arm up over the back of a theater seat for an hour. It really wasn't so bad once the shoulder went numb. I guess a five second kiss goodnight was worth that small sacrifice.

1968, at age 18 I thought I had them figured out. They could manipulate the boys into doing whatever they wanted to and the magic weapon they used was that dress that had been getting even smaller. Gentlemen, do you remember the dresses they wore in 1968. I know every one of you know what I am talking about when I say "Daisy Dukes", don't you? I thought it was a boys thing until I watched a few of those girls around their dads. Dads were worse than the boys. You've heard the expression, "Girls want to marry someone just like their dad". That's why, because girls could make them do anything they wanted also. The mystery still existed; why do they still cry at the drop of a hat?

I met and married my "First Girl" in 1970. We were, and still are so in Love. I thought if I had one at home I could figure out the crying thing that was going on with them. Seems as though they cry when they are sad, cry when they are happy, and cry while watching movies. It was getting worse.

In 1974 my wife Colette gave me my "Second Girl", Amy. She came out of the womb crying and didn't stop for four months. They called it colic. I called it catching up. Two years later, here came my "Third Girl", Marsha. I thought I had a special one here, she wasn't crying as much. I thought I might have discovered something here with two little ones. Amy and Marsha loved playing with each other and the house was much quieter, except for when Colette was watching a movie. About one year after Marsha was born, she discovered she had her own toys and didn't want Amy to play with them. I tried buying things like kitchen play sets to make them think it was for both. Then one would claim the pots and one would claim the pans.

When they became teenagers it was all becoming clearer. They could handle the boys like a couple of champs and they had figured out where dad's button was also. They could roll them big eyes up at me and I could feel my wallet creeping out of my back pocket by itself.

I walked them down the aisle a few months apart and it broke my heart to give them up. They both were very lucky when their children starting coming. They both had two "Boys" each. Lucky rascals!

After more than fifty years of trying to figure girls out and I am no further than the first day of school. I do know my three girls have changed my life completely. And when I think of them, I find myself crying!

Thanks Girls, you've made me a woman…

"A bank is a place that will lend you money, if you can prove that you don't need it".
bob hope

Pole Road...

I grew up in the area between Portageville and Clarkton Missouri. This area was called the East Swamp. Cypress trees rose eighty feet above the swamp. Cotton mouth snakes wrapped their shiny bodies around clumps of pigweed; wild grapevines dangled like thick ropes from the canopy. A black curly moss grew in patches on the damp soil thus giving it the name "wool swamp." The cypress of this great virgin forest had never felt the bite of a pioneer axe until the 1800s. Birds filled the air; turtles, frogs, and snakes were thick in the water; panthers and bears prowled the shores.

It was very difficult to cross the swamp. Canoe trails had been marked on fallen trees pointing directions like modern signs. What was needed, however, was a dry road from Portageville to Clarkton. One day a mare and her colt escaped from a pen near the town of Weaversville, which is near Portageville. The owner tracked the mare and colt into the swamp through present-day Gideon and up to Bach, which is now Clarkton. Many people thought the path that the mare and colt took was the best way through the swamp. They created a "dump" road--a road that is built up higher than the surrounding swamp land. People thought a more permanent road would be better. In the mid 1850s a man named Major Henry E. Clark built a plank road. This plank road was a toll road. Prices for crossing were:

   $2.00 for wagons going west
   1.25 for regular freight wagons
   .75 for horseback
   .10 for walking

The plank road served the area well until the Civil War years. In 1862 a Union detachment came up to a cabin just east of Clarkton. Inside were Home Guards sipping on whiskey in front of a fire. One of the men suddenly announced, "I smell a yankee." Moments later the Union detachments fired a few cannon shots into Clarkton. On their way back to New Madrid, the Union soldiers burned large sections of the Plank Road and the bridges so guerillas and confederates could not use the road to follow them.

The residents of Clarkton, Portageville and other surrounding communities wanted the road rebuilt. Funding was difficult, so instead of planks they patched the road with poles. Thereafter, people called it the Pole Road. This road is now known as highway 162.

Founding of Gideon, Missouri…

It was a small clearing in a swamp of towering trees. Frank and Pauling Noisworthy owned most of this land inhabited mainly by deer, wild hogs, opossums, coons, wildcats, and bears. There were no highways or drainage ditches. There were only the forest, washouts, sloughs, and a pole road connecting this tiny clearing with Point Pleasant and Cape Girardeau. One could hardly imagine what this area would be in the years to come.

In 1899, F. E. Gideon from Ohio and W.P. Anderson from Indiana came to the southeast of Missouri on a hunting trip. While hunting they noticed the vast virgin forest and the fertile soil and began thinking of the possibilities for a prosperous lumber business. When they returned home, they discussed with other interested parties the possibilities of expanding the lumber business to southeast Missouri.

Then in 1900 W. P. Anderson and his brother M. S. Anderson, of Indiana, F. E. Gideon, and M. V. Mumma of Ohio came to this part of Missouri to engage in the lumber business. They wanted to locate in either Clarkton or Malden but neither town would permit the building of the mill. They decided to built the mill in the forest where the timber was located. They bought the first tract of land, as well as later tracts of land, from Frank Noisworthy of Clarkton. In 1901 a partnership was organized by W.P. Anderson, M.S. Anderson, M.V. Mumma, F.E. Gideon, and a Mr. Snyder. This partnership was called the Clarkton Lumber Company. In 1907 the Clarkton Lumber Company was reorganized and incorporated as the Gideon-Anderson Lumber and Mercantile Company. It was purchased in 1911 by the Gideon/Anderson Lumber and Mercantile Company and its name changed to the Gideon Cooperage Company; it was discontinued in 1942. In 1901 this lumber company, named the Clarkton Lumber Company, began forming the community of Gideon, complete with two stores, a charcoal factory, and a railroad. Mr. Gideon retained his residence in Ohio until about 1905, when he and Mrs. Gideon moved to Gideon and resided here until 1908. In 1908 he sold his interest in the Gideon-Anderson Company to the other stockholders and returned to his home at McGill, Ohio. Mr. Gideon died at his home in McGill, Ohio in 1919.

Early settlers began coming into the community looking for work and places to settle. Most of the workers were employed at the Gideon-Anderson Lumber Company or Gideon North Island Railroad, which was built in 1903.

Go Fishing…

There are a lot of reasons why people go fishing. Some fish for the pleasure they get from it, others fish for a living , and some fish for food. Of all these reasons, fishing for pleasure is definitely the most enjoyable. See, fishing for fun is simply a personal choice. Just something you want to do. There is no stress in fishing for the fun of it. You don't get in trouble for not catching anything. You might be a little disappointed, but that's it. Besides the pleasure of actually catching fish, there are lots more benefits in fishing. Most of these are good for your physical as well as your mental health.

Physically, fishing is not all that tough on you. You don't need a great deal of strength and stamina. But, it will exercise your lungs, heart and several other muscle groups. After all, you do have to get to a location where you fish. Most of the time this includes walking, maybe climbing, plus you have to carry your gear to your favorite fishing hole. These are all physical activities and you will burn calories getting there. All of these things are good for your health. The many things you have to do to get ready to go fishing are also a good workout for the muscles of the fingers, hands, wrists and arms. Putting your rod and reel together, attaching hooks, sinkers, floaters and even in some cases digging your bait are all activities which work several muscles. Let's not forget there is the casting your bait into the water. This works out your muscles of the upper arm, shoulder and back. You are probably not going to get a good cardio workout from fishing, unless you are fishing in stumps or lillie pads and stay hung up most of the time.

Fishing is also excellent for the lungs and skin. Think about it, fishing is mostly an outdoor sport. Being outdoors gives you an opportunity to get plenty of fresh air into your lungs. Fresh air is good air. It contains plenty of oxygen which is basic to a healthier physical and mental state. Sunshine is another health benefit that comes from fishing. There are lots of people that like fishing enough to even go in bad weather, however, most prefer a nice sunny day to fish. Sunshine, in moderation, is great for your health. It provides several beneficial attributes for maintaining a healthy body and good looks.

Mentally, fishing for fun takes little or no effort. Just bait your hook, toss it into the water, and wait for the fish to come by and take it. That doesn't sound too hard does it? Of course not, and that is the greatest of all benefits to your health you can get. Fishing doesn't take a lot of brain power, therefore, all your brain cells get a chance to kick back and relax. Fishing lets you rest and relax your mind. No stress, no cell phones, nobody wanting this or that, no noisy machines or people; just good old clean fresh air, some great sunshine and plenty of rest. Allows your brain to take a small vacation! However, you shouldn't get too relaxed, just in case something big grabs your bate and takes off with it. Just remember to pack a couple of good ole healthy fried bologna sandwiches, jug of coffee, and a pair of candy bars. Fresh air, sunshine and exercise usually improves your appetite, so it is always a good idea to take some kind of "pleasure" food on any fishing trip.

To wrap this up, it should be pretty obvious by now that fishing is a great recipe for a healthier mind and body. Take a little exercise, add some fresh air, good snacks along with your favorite soft drink to wash it down with. Now if you do this as often as you can, who knows how long you might live. If god forbid should decide to take you early, just know, the time spent here on earth fishing will be much improved. Lastly, with a little luck, you might catch a stringer full of fish for dinner, and everyone knows that eating fish is very healthy. Enjoy your Summer, Go Fishing!

"My husband wanted one of those big-screen TVs for his birthday. So I just moved his chair closer to the one we have already".

wendy liebman

Go get me some onions…

My granny and grandpa, P.O. and Dollie Beasley raised me from the time I was four years old until I graduated from high school in 1968. Grandpa P.O. was a no nonsense farmer who worked from daylight til dark every week day and half day on Saturday. He then drank Colonel Lee whisky from noon on Saturday til Sunday morning. Waking up bright and early Sunday morning he would not stop pestering me and my Granny until we called all of his kids and told him they where coming for Sunday dinner.

He had already raised eight kids and still had three at home when I came along. Fortunately for me, he was tired spanking children. I was happy for that. It meant he really didn't want to bother spanking me. I only remember him spanking me twice. He left the discipline up to my Granny. I could usually hug my way out of trouble with her. I remember one time when I was around 10 years old, I brought a rope I found across the road at the rodeo corral into the living room. She kept telling me to get it back outside where it belonged. I was sitting on the couch with the rope behind me when she had finally had enough of my silliness and jerked it from behind me causing a nice little rope burn on my lower back. Now I can't remember everything that happened! I sometimes still get faint thinking about it. I might have overplayed that incident… until I was about thirty years old. She felt so bad, she never spanked me again after that.

We were having a nice Sunday dinner one August day with the dinner table full of garden vegetables and a big bowl of Fried chicken. My Grandpa was sitting in his "place" at the head of the table and I was sitting to his right side of the table near the other end. He told me to run out to the garden and get him some fresh onions. There was a small bowl of fresh onions right in front of me, but were hidden from his view by a larger bowl of mashed taters. I decided to be a comedian and said "Go get your own!" Now, remember, when I said my Grandpa only spanked me twice that I recall; This was the first time! Up from the table he jumped and in two steps he was standing at the back door, with it open. I, however had moved back to the bathroom door waiting for his next move. For just an instant, I thought he was having a little fun at my expense, but I was terribly wrong. I dropped to my knees and tried to crawl through his legs and escape to the outside where I could probably outrun him. I managed to crawl half way through his legs. He closed his legs on both sides of my waist and locked me solid with my butt right in front of him.

Let's just say at this point, all the fun went out of it for me. From that day forward I made absolutely sure there were fresh onions directly in front of my Grandpa P.O. totally unobstructed.

Going Back Home…

My wife Colette and I just finished watching a movie called "Trip to Bountiful". The film, set in the 1940s, tells the story of an elderly woman who wants to return home to the small town where she grew up but an overprotective son would not let her travel alone.

She was determined to outwit her son and bossy daughter-in-law, and sets out to board a bus to a town near her childhood home. On the journey, she befriends a girl traveling alone and reminisces about her younger years and grieves for her lost relatives. Her son and daughter-in-law eventually track her down, with the help of the local country police chief. However, she is determined and the local sheriff, moved by her yearning to visit her childhood home, offers to drive her out to what remains of her hometown community of Bountiful, deserted, and the few remaining houses are derelict. She is moved to tears as she surveys her father's land and the remains of the family home. Her son eventually turns up, and drives her back to Houston.

As we watched the show, I began to wonder how great it would be to return to my childhood home for a day. To sit on the front porch with a warm summer breeze blowing through the cottonwood trees and listen to the sounds of the birds, crickets, and the frogs singing in the road ditch in front of the house. To hear that old John Deere tractor back fire when my Grandpa P.O. Beasley drove up from the field for dinner. The smells of beans and cornbread, cabbage, fried chicken cooking in the kitchen and a big apple pie cooling in the kitchen window.

What would it be like to open the front door to the living room with the pot-bellied stove setting on the square metal sheet to keep it from burning the linoleum rug. To set on the boxed-shaped vinyl couch and look over at the matching vinyl chair with a tear from my Grandpa sitting in it with a screwdriver in his back pocket. The hole was enlarged from sitting in the chair and it had cotton stuffing sticking out of it. On the other side of the room was the Philco black and white TV that got two channels if the weather was good, channels 6 and 12. To again walk through my old bedroom heading to the kitchen and see my iron bedstead setting in the corner, next to the open window with a hole in the screen where I use to lay awake at night watching lightening bugs fly by. The window where I saw the pump house burn down late one night. Across the hall was my Aunt Margie's bedroom. I didn't dare go in there without permission. I do have a picture of eight of us bed in that room.

How I could leave my old bedroom where the homemade wooden shelves held the fruit jars full of canned goods covered by an old sheet and walk into the kitchen where I would see my Granny Beasley standing at the stove stirring a skillet of white gravy humming amazing grace. She would be wearing that same print apron she had for twenty plus years. The old chrome dining room table with the Formica top surrounded by four chrome chairs covered in light yellow vinyl decorated with chrome thumb tacks around the edges would be covered with food no matter which meal was being served.

In the Southwest corner of the kitchen was an unpainted bathroom which had just been installed to replace the old outhouse out in the back yard. Grandpa didn't use that bathroom for the first year it was built, something about old dogs and new tricks. The bad part about the indoor bathroom was the "bath" part. Granny expected me to bathe two to three times a week. You can rub your skin off doing that.

Stepping out on the back porch I would meet Grandpa P.O. slapping the field dust off of his overalls from the mornings plowing with his cap. He would step over to the wash tub full of rinse water from the load of clothes Granny finished just before making dinner and wash his hands and face. Grabbing the hand towel hanging on a nail by the back door, drying his face and hands as he went in the house to lunch.

I looked through the window and saw my Grandpa walk over and give my Granny a kiss on the cheek and say something I couldn't hear. I am sure it was "I Love You". Not something you would see and hear but maybe once in your lifetime.

I would turn and look out across the back yard past the chicken coop where I must have fed a thousand chickens during my stay there, past the smokehouse where a couple of big old hams hang wrapped in a burlap sack covered in curing salt, out into the field of young cotton plants trying to grow in the hottest gumbo there was.

As my mind wondered back to today and I came back from my trip back home, the movie ended. I will have to watch that movie again to see what happened to her on her trip back home!

"The shinbone is a device for finding furniture in a dark room".
anonymous

Good ole days…

My name is Terry Weldon and I grew up in Gideon Missouri. I lived there from the time I was born in 1950 the day after high school graduation in 1968. Looking back it was such a short period of time, however, it made the biggest impression on my life than any of the next 45 years since then. I have always heard about the "Good Ole Days", but I never could pin them down. I have enjoyed my life thus far, joining the Air Force, getting married, having three children and watching them grow into fine adults. But, we usually refer to our childhood years as "The Good Ole Days". I think it was because there was something about the unknown. We didn't know what to expect around every corner and that was the adrenalin rush we enjoyed when we were young. It might have been because we were the smartest during our childhood years.

I remember when I was a pre-teen and like most, I was smarter than the average bear. There was very little I didn't know. When I hit my teen years, like most of the boys I went to school with, I was near-genius. You couldn't tell me anything I didn't already know. I married at the age of twenty and my new bride thought I hung the moon. I could do no wrong. Going into my twenties with children being born, I had a few years of just knowing almost everything again. Once the children began to ask questions, I again was a genius, or at least they thought I was.

My thirty something years when the kids were becoming teenagers, I started going down-

 hill, I mean I was pretty stupid for a few years. The kids began graduating and leaving home at which time my IQ creeped upward a few points. That was kind of a tough few years with the kids at home thinking I was a total idiot and the one that moved out of the house thinking I might have half a brain.

Finally, all of the kids had graduated and left home, the nest was empty and I was not so smart any longer. I was now "Wiser". Just when I thought I had it all back and could focus on my retirement years as a "Wise old Man", my wife's view of me changed somewhere around forty years of marriage. I again, was an idiot! How did this all happen. I have no idea and I am no longer smart enough to figure it out…

"The best time to give advice to your children is while they're still young enough to believe you know what you're talking about".

evan esar

Grandpas Overalls...

Many men, almost all of the "old school" farmers wore Bib overalls. They were very comfortable for men with an "extended" belly. Bib overalls were pants from the ankles to the waist, and a Bib for the upper body. They are worn with a shirt underneath the bib. Most of them had buttons to close the waist which was sometimes left unbuttoned, sorta like an air conditioner. They also had buckles to hold them on the shoulders. They had lots of different size pockets. One on the chest which held a wallet two small ones for a pencil and a much desired pocket watch. Oversized back pockets for anything you needed to put in them, usually some kind of tool. There were a couple odd shaped pockets on one leg where a folding carpenter's ruler was suppose to go, but, my Grandpa put his snuff can in it. On the other leg there was a "hammer loop" for the carpenter. After they had been washed a few times they were softer and more comfortable to wear. They are comfortable because their roomy fit allows for easy movement. Along with their strong construction and durable fabric, the bib style protected clothing and skin from spills, cuts and hazardous working conditions.

Overalls are made in many colors. They were white for painters, blue for farmers, and pinstripes for railroad workers.

Created sometime in the 1700s, they were known as slops. They were made for the working man. They were cheap and considered to be for the lower class. In the beginning they were very durable, not made for comfort, and didn't fit very well. Many men wore them over another pair of pants and took them off before leaving work. As run-of-the-mill slops were not ideal for many workers, some changes had to be made. This included better fit and pockets. Around the 1850s, manufacturers started making them out of denim.

On the farm, and in blue-collar occupations, by the 1930s and 1940s, blue denim bib overalls competed for popularity with Levi jeans. I remember my Grandpa always had a pocket watch attached with a leather braided chain looped through the eyelet and neatly tucked in one of his smallest bib pocket. His pocket knife, snuff box, a pencil stub, handkerchief, nuts, bolts along with a couple of different tools — and maybe a block of "Bull-of-the-Woods" chewing tobacco could be found in one of the many pockets.

Although overalls were a favorite among most farmers, their young teenage sons did not care for them. They considered them "Grandpa" clothes and were strictly for working on the farm, fields and factories. Because they were economical and durable, some young men were forced to wear them to school. In order to put their own twist on them, some boys would unbuckle one of their suspenders in order to add a little "Style" to them.

Overalls were perfect for rough and tough toddlers and young boys. Moms liked them because they were economical and tough. Little boys, unlike their teenage brothers enjoyed dressing like grandpa. OshKosh overalls are still very popular for children today.

Something happened when the bib overalls moved from the farms, and factories onto the main streets in the 1960s. Some of the high-dollar retailers began making them out of a higher quality fabric and in many different colors. By the 1990s, hip-hop artists wore bib overalls with one strap unbuttoned. This began a trend that spread across America like a wildfire. It was the thing to wear in most high schools.

Around 2008 many female celebrities began wearing denim skirts with a bib overall top, showing that they were not just for the working man. Plaid and patterned overalls began to show up in them fancy-smancy boutiques, and as fads go, people bought them just to show off their high-dollar labels.

While bib overalls are still widely used by painters, farmers, mechanics and carpenters, they are a long way from their original design and now can be purchased anywhere.

Wrangler was the first company to manufacture bib overalls. A company called Big Smith has been making them for more than 80 years and are the largest supplier of bib overalls in the world. There are more than 42 brands made with only a few of them in the United States.

If you are from my neck of the woods, they are known as "Over-Halls" Not sure how that came about. I still have a pair of my Grandpas Overalls.

No matter what design you see or wear, the best remembered will always be those that Grandpa wore for they were the ones that were full of hard work, all sorts of gadgets, and most of all, they were full of "Grandpa".

"The odds of going to the store for a loaf of bread and coming out with only a loaf of bread are three billion to one".

erma bombeck

Grocery Money...

From the time I was about ten years old til about fifteen years old it was my job to bring home the grocery money. That seems a little young for being the bread winner, well here is how I did it.

My Grandpa P.O. Beasley was a hard working sharecropper all of his life and his boss never had to tell him when to be at work and when to quit. It was simple for him, if the sun was up, you should be at work, if the Gideon Box Plant whistle blew, it was five o'clock and he went home. Even a half mile away with the tractor running you could hear that whistle. Grandpa worked five and a half days a week on the farm and I never saw him take a drink of anything but water while at work and mostly sweet tea at home. However, come Saturday at noon, he would park that tractor in the corner of the yard, go in the house, take a bath, take off his dirty overalls and put on a clean pair. (Why call them a pair of overalls when they were one piece?). By the time he was finished and dressed, I would have his shaving mug and razor ready on the front porch where I gave him a nice clean shave for fifty cents. This would get me in the Malden theater and get me popcorn and a sodie.

After Grandpa was shaven he headed for down town Gideon Missouri, particularly, Gibb's Bar. Upon entering Gibb's he would walk straight to the bar where Gibbs would hand him two half pints of Colonel Lee whisky. He would open one and drink down in one gulp and slip the second bottle in his back pocket. Then he would go out to the front of Gibb's to sit with the other elderly gentlemen of the town on what we called "Spit and Whittle Corner". There were steps at the entrance of the Bar with an eight foot benches on both sides of the steps. Both benches were usually full by this time.

The activities going on at these benches were somewhat less than honest when it came to "knife swapping". No not "Wife Swapping"; that was the next generation! For some unknown reason this generation thought one of the rights to manhood was to have the sharpest knife in town. I was always amazed by the fact that each man on those benches had at least two knives on him at any given time, one to show how sharp he could make it, and the other to swap. Now, here is how the swapping took place. First, two gentlemen would bring out the knife they had been sharpening for ten minutes, (every man on that bench had his own whit rock in his pocket to sharpen his knives), for you city folk, that was a small sharpening stone. Anyway, both gentlemen interested in swapping knives would first show how sharp his knife was by shaving the hair on his arm, not all of the hair, just enough to prove his point. Just looking at the old men's arms was pretty funny with several patches of hair shaved off on all of them. OK, Back to the swap. If either one of the men had to scrap the knife blade more than once to remove the patch of hair, the other gentleman got the choice of swapping or not. For example, you scrapped the patch of hair on your arm and it came off nice and clean, however I had to scrap twice, you won the right to decide if you wanted to swap knives after you presented them to each other.

Right along here Grandpa would stop to take a "break". He would go back into the bar, walk through and out the back door to what was known as the "Bull Pen". No, there were no baseball players warming up and no bulls back there either, even though it did smell like it most of the time.

The bull pen was the back yard for the bar and it had a privacy fence on both sides running back to the side walls of Dye's barber shop. The only way in or out of the bull pen was through Gibb's bar. This area was extremely important to the bar's patrons because Gibb's had no restroom. Therefore, this is where the gentlemen "relieved" themselves. So, Grandpa went to the edge of the porch and, well, you get the picture…

It had been about thirty minutes since Grandpa had chugged the first half pint. When he was finished with "his business", he took the bottle from his back pocket, opened it and down it went in maybe two gulps. He would stop and purchase two more half pints, one for each back pocket, on his way back to the bench out front.

Now every man on spit and whittle corner new there was going to be a "swap" and they were all paying close attention to this event. Once the decision was made as to who could say yes or no to the knife swap, the two gentlemen would put those knives back in their pocket because they would never swap their sharp knives. They would reach in the other pocket, pull out a "swapping" knife, keeping it palms down so the other gentlemen cannot see it. Both gents dropped their knife into the other ones hand at the same time. Most of the time, these two knives weren't worth ten cents. Most were rusty, handles missing or blades broken, may have been one they found in the field where it had been buried for twenty years. That was the fun of the knife swapping game. To see who could come up with the worst knife and pawn it off on some other sucker. The sharp knife competition had nothing to do with it whatsoever!

Now another thirty minutes has passed and Grandpa has felt the "urge" again to visit the bull pen. This time he chugs his third half pint, then takes care of his business. There were usually two or three other fellas in the bull pen feeling no pain at this point in the day. Grandpa would sit down on the back steps and shoot the breeze with one or two of them, by this time the conversations were not very coherent on either side and after a few minutes both men would fall silent, lean back against the wall to soak in the afternoon sunshine. They were already pretty warm on the inside, now the outside was getting there and the sandman was right behind them sprinkling fairy dust all over the back porch of Gibb's bar.

This is where I came in. My job, per Granny Beasley, was to go through Grandpa's billfold and take all of his money but three dollars. I was usually next door at Dye's pool hall or the City Café. I knew he was about ripe for the picking so I would go down to Gibb's, walk to the back porch where I would find him "enjoying" the afternoon. Because Grandpa wore overalls, it was easy to access his billfold simply by unsnapping the bib and taking the billfold out, never waking him. Usually this would be perceived as theft in most parts of the country, however, everyone in town new exactly what I was doing and no one ever said a word. Truth be told, I probably wasn't the only boy doing this behind Gibbs on a Saturday afternoon. Making sure I took all but three dollars, I would take the rest home to Granny Beasley because it was my job to bring home the Grocery money. Not exactly what you expected when you began reading this, was it?

"Life expectancy would grow by leaps and bounds if green vegetables smelled as good as bacon".

doug larson

Help a brother out...

My mother, Joe BEASLEY Weldon had multiple sclerosis and passed away at the age of twenty nine in 1954. She was in a wheelchair for the last few years of her life. I was four years old when she passed and I don't remember much about her. I remember that she had a big collie dog that stayed underneath her wheelchair. I often wondered how it kept from getting it's tail ran over, but it didn't. I also remember that mom had a hair brush that she kept tucked away by her leg. When me or my brother, Jack (Puncho) or my sister, Patricia (Sissie) did something we shouldn't have done, she would call us to come to her for our punishment. We had a great deal of respect for our mom, or we weren't too bright and didn't hesitate to go right over to her take our punishment from the back of that brush on our little behinds. She would probably get in trouble today for using the hairbrush on us. Some sort of child abuse. I personally think we need a lot more hair brushes being used in this country now days.

Mom would make all of our clothes using my Granny Beasley's treadle sewing machine. Because her legs had drawn up in the chair from the multiple sclerosis, she would turn the sewing machine with her hand on top. Sometimes one of us children would lie underneath her and peddle for her. I still don't know how she managed it.

I think it was the mailman, who was either a journalist for our local paper, or just loved to gossip passed the word around town about mom and how she was a single mom, making her children's clothes trying to survive. Some of the town's people got together and bought mom a new electric sewing. She was as proud as a peacock and although I don't remember, I suspect we kids had lots of new clothes for a while.

While the rest of the family worked in the cotton fields every year, mom would cook and care for the house when she was able. Me, my brother and sister were too young to be in the fields working, so we were home with mom. I was too little to do much, but my brother Puncho was just the right age to do everything from, climbing into the cabinets and retrieving pots, pans, and bowels to going out into the garden for vegetables.

One day, Puncho, who was around eight years old was really busy doing tasks for mom and I felt a little sorry for him. Mom told him to take the trash can out of the kitchen, dump it into the burning barrel and burn it. He whimpered a little about how much he was having to do, Sissie was a girl and they didn't do trash back then, and I was too small do it and mom wouldn't tell me too. He was complaining and saying that it just wasn't fair. Mom was off in the bedroom sewing and Sissie was out on the front porch playing with a doll or something, so I decided I would give him a hand. I was around four years old and couldn't pick the trash can up to take it out side and burn the trash, so I set the trash can on fire in the kitchen! Made perfect sense when I was four…

His eyes shined…

I have a friend from my hometown, Gideon, Missouri who began to put his memories in short stories. I enjoyed reading those stories, because I could relate to them so, I thought I could try my hand at it.

When my wife and I, along with our three children were in the USAF, stationed at Nellis AFB, NV, between 1977 and 1983 we wanted to do everything we could to teach our three children, some might say, to the point of being obsessed, right and wrong. I was a disciplinarian, which is effective, but may not be the best child rearing method.

I was a Scoutmaster, Webelos leader, couched Tee ball and soccer all at the same time for several years trying to involve our children in good, clean, wholesome activities.

One summer we were having an "Arrow of Light" ceremony out in the Valley of Fire state park. We spent hours setting up campsites, preparing the props to be used for the ceremony and trying to remember our lines for the presentation. There were five boys who had worked very hard to earn the highest award you can receive in the Cub Scouts. One of the boys to receive the award that night was my son, Jeff Weldon. I had pushed him hard to get to this point in his Scouting career and I remember thinking about how to present these awards without showing more pride for Jeff's achievement than the other boys.

The sun was setting and we gathered all of the Scouts and their families around what was soon to be our campfire set against a thirty foot flat rock wall that will reflect the campfire perfectly. We brought out the American flag, said our pledge, and was ready to start the campfire. The setting sun shined over to the top of the next thirty foot tall rock where an Indian warrior came up from the back of the rock, raised his bow, released a flaming arrow, (on a wire) which landed right in the center of the "friendship fire". The fire was roaring to life in seconds. Perfect in every way. Everyone there was awe-struck. Looking back to the top of the rock and the Indian had vanished into the night.

After the oooing and awing finally subsided, I began explaining about all of the badges the boys had earned to get to the "Arrow of Light". Calling the boys up to the campfire one at a time, everything went flawlessly. I began to start the closing ceremony when I realized I had forgotten to present the award to my own son. I was more than embarrassed. Jeff took it in stride, but I saw it in his eyes, they were sad, I had hurt his feelings. We called him up, made some silly comment about the situation and presented his award.

A few weeks later Jeff and I were working on his Pinewood Derby car for the big Cub Scout annual races. We were together in the back yard, one on one working diligently to get it just right. He was explaining to me why red, white, and blue were the best colors for his car. I turned, looked down at him and I saw it in his eyes, they were shining, all he ever cared about was simply being with me.

Looking back at my actions in trying to do what I thought was best for my children, I probably neglected them more than I helped them. I wish I had those days back. I would do things a little differently, but wouldn't we all.

"I grew up with six brothers. That's how I learned to dance

-waiting for the bathroom".

bob hope

I smell a snake…

I have a cousin, Freddie Layne, who swore he could smell a snake if one was anywhere around us. Of course, we thought he was a little silly at the time, but one July night in 1966 he made a believer out of me and several other cousins that were with us. The family had all gathered over at my cousin Sonny Kilgo's house near Risco Missouri for some special family event. I can't remember what it was, but like most people in Southeast Missouri, we didn't need much of a reason to get together and eat.

After supper there were several cousins out in the backyard swatting mosquitoes and telling tales when Fred came up with the fact that he could smell a snake if it were in his local area. We all had a good laugh. I told them if I were with Sonny Kilgo I knew if there was a snake near us because I could smell Sonny, cause he liked them as much as I do!

I, for one, am petrified of snakes, doesn't matter what kind they are, how big or small they are, I simply can't handle them. There were a few cousins that had no fear of them at all, but most were as scared of them as I am.

It was nearing sunset that evening and we were snooping around in Uncle Cecil Kilgo's tractor shed where we found about fifteen to twenty fishing poles all wadded in the corner. We picked out the one we wanted to fish with, took it outside, cleaned it a little, threw it out a few times to make sure the fishing line was still good.

Living out in the country, Uncle Cecil had the drain for his kitchen sink and washing machine draining just passed his back yard. As all men from that are knew that was the perfect place to dig up fishing worms. A couple of cousins were digging us up some bait while the others got the poles ready. We walked down the gravel road to number four ditch bridge to see if we could catch a few catfish. The bridge was an old iron rail bridge that looked like a railroad trestle with board runners for the cars to cross over on. We lined up on the bridge and dropped our lines in the ditch and went back to telling our tales. It was just about dark and after a minute or two someone caught a nice catfish. There were about six of us fishing and not one thought to bring a fish stringer. Fred tramples off down the ditch bank. You couldn't have paid me to go down there. He stirred around in the weeds and reached down to bring up some sort of heavy vine, fashioned a stringer and strung up the catfish, staked it out on the bank and just sat down right there in the weeds. I said, "let me know if you smell any snakes down there", we all had a laugh and kept fishing. After a minute or two Fred shouted up to us to shine the flashlight down his way in the ditch, that he smelled a snake. We shined the light in the middle of the ditch and sure enough, there was a snake swimming down the ditch. We laughed and said in this particular ditch you could see a snake every minute if you looked around. There were another couple of catfish caught up on the bridge and of course, me being the smallest of the group, I had to take it down for Fred to add it to the stringer. Reluctantly, I eased down the back with one eye watching the path I was walking on and the other eye doing a 360 degree look around the snake infested area.

There were a few more catfish caught and I decided to just sit down with Fred and let someone else bring them down to us. Fred turned to me and said, "I smell another one". I was becoming a believer, so I stood up, shined the light around and there it was on the other bank slithering up into the weeds. At this point, if Fred were an evangelist, I would have started sending him money!

As darkness fell upon us and the fish were beginning to quit biting, we just talked and teased each other for a while longer, (one of those great times you look back on and were just glad you were there). The mosquitoes had found out where we were and we were all starting to look like we had chicken pox. Just as we were talking about going back to the house, Fred said, "Boys I smell a snake and he is close"! Well, me being a devout believer, I shined the light all over that ditch bank, but could see nothing. Fred insisted it was close and I wasn't doubting him for a second. I suggested we get the fish and head back. He grabbed the stringer and brought out a nice stringer of 8 to 10 catfish, of which the one on the bottom of the stringer had a nice water moccasin hanging on it. Fred, being one of those that didn't fear snakes, reached down and grabbed that snake behind the head, pulled it off that catfish and said, "here, hold this"!

I had just finished a plate of peach cobbler when the rest of them got back to the house! Fred said, "I meant hold the stringer".

Love them Mulberries…

Back in the early to mid 1960s, there was a field road where our driveway was. When you turned into our driveway you could turn left into our yard or continue down to the end of the field road to a little unpainted farm house. This little farm house had old torn window dressings if any at all. There was a chicken coop and two trees in the yard, one of which was a large mulberry tree. They had no grass in the yard and there was either mulberry stains or bird droppings all over the yard.

The old gentleman that lived there then was named Jeff Waddles. His wife lived with him and I think her name was Bell, but I am not sure, you know for American men your memory is the second thing to go! He was a large man and he scared me and all my friends, just by looking at him. One day me and my cousin, Lonnie Jr Beasley were playing up and down the field road, riding our stick horses and hard as we could. He had a strawberry roan and I had an appaloosa. They were fine looking steeds and could run like the wind. We had ridden them down to the Waddles house one day and noticed there was no one home. We rode up to the house to give our horses a drink as they were all lathered up from running so hard and we could use a drink too. They had a square box built around there pump in the back yard near their back porch. There was a pan on the box for washing up in. We pumped some water in it and sat it in the yard, placed our stick horses heads in it and let them drink. He pumped while I drank and I pumped while he drank. It was crystal clear and cold well water. The kind you don't see any more in this country.

We heard and saw Mr Waddles coming home on the tractor and decided we didn't want to be seen riding our horses away from his house, so we ran to the chicken house to hide until he went in his house, then we could sneak away back home. As we started to open the coop door we frightened the chicken and they scrambled around the yard cackling. We decided that we would not be able to sneak out without doing the same thing to the chickens and that wouldn't work. We then both ran to the mulberry tree, which was easier to climb. We shimmed up the tree taking our horses with us. We climb a little more than half way up the mulberry tree by the time Mr Waddles drove into the driveway to park the tractor. We froze where we were and I am sure I was breathing about three breathes per minute and I don't think Lonnie Jr breathed at all. Mr Waddles climbed down from the tractor and dusted off his overalls from driving all day in a self made dust storm. He was stiff from sitting on that 'A' model John Deere that had very little seat cover left on it and half of the black from the steering wheel gone completely. He slowly walked over to the water pump, noticed the pan in the yard, yelled out at his wife for leaving it there. The wind might come along and blow it away into the field. He spouted that he wasn't made of money, sat the pan into the hole cutout on the box under the pump. He pumped it about half full, walked over to the back porch, picked up a cake of lye soap and towel and wash rag. He returned to the pump, unstapped the galluses on his overalls and flipped them over his shoulders, dropped the bib and pulled off his shirt. I was beginning to wonder exactly what I was going to see that evening, but he stopped there, soaped up the wash rag with the lye soap and began to wash his upper body. We were still trying to hold our breathes without being noticed. He was always yelling at us to stay out of the mulberry trees and the thought of him catching us red handed in his tree was almost more than I could wrap my head around. After he washed and dried off, he pulled the bib of his overalls up, connected the galluses and poured the pan of water out in the yard where the grassless soil sucked it up in seconds. He replaced the pan, headed for the chicken house stirred around in there for three or four minutes while Lonnie Jr and I hung on to those limbs with every muscle in our butt cheeks. Finally, Mr Waddles came out of the chicken house with five or six eggs wrapped in the towel he just used to dry off with. As the sun was turning orange, getting ready to set, Mr Waddles stepped up on his back porch, opened the door, turned back to the Mulberry tree and shouted, "you boys get on down out of that mulberry tree and get on home before it gets dark"! Then he went on in his house to eat supper…

Me and Dan...

Growing up in a family of ten Aunts and Uncle, I had lots of cousins and I was very close to all of them. Each relationship was different. Danny Beasley was one that was like a brother. We spent most weekends together either at their house or ours. One weekend Danny was spending the night with me and we had made us a campfire in the back yard near the smoke house. We were sharper
than most boys our age and we had, earlier that day, soaked several corncobs in a pan of gasoline to help them burn better in the campfire, (you can already see we were pretty sharp!). Thinking like a true boy scout, I had placed the pan just under the edge of the smokehouse to keep it away from the fire. As Danny and I sat by the fire talking about the week's events and what we were going to do after we were done being astronauts, he would place the tip of a long stick he had in the gasoline and them light it over the fire. I'm pretty sure he was chasing bugs with the flame on the tip of the stick.. After a stream of gasoline had built up between the pan and the fire, it finally lit, running straight to the pan of gas, and up it went, setting just under the edge of the smokehouse. Being afraid it would burn the smokehouse down, I grab the handle of the pan and attempted to toss it over the garden fence where it would do no damage. The handle on the old pan was hallow and worn, causing the pan to spin upside down and pour the gasoline all over my me from the waist down. In an instant I was a ball of fire. Danny took off running into the house, while I decided to

head for the road ditch which was full from the rain we had earlier that day. We were in the back yard and the ditch was in front of our house, so, as I began to run, the flames got even higher. Knowing pretty quickly this wasn't going to work, I looked for some other way to put out the fire, I spotted the water faucet at the edge of the back porch and decided to get under it and turn on the water, as I squatted and turned on the water, Danny came running out of the house with a blanket from the bed. He jumped me like a flea on a hound dog. For a moment I am sure we looked like a midget wrestling team rolling all over the back yard. After the fire was out he told me he had learned in cub scouts earlier that week to wrap the victim in a blanket and that is what he was going to do. I was burned pretty bad on both legs and missed working in the fields that summer, which didn't break my heart, however I also missed playing baseball that summer and that did upset me. Looking back, I've often wondered how bad I would have gotten burned, if Dan hadn't rolled me up in the blanket.

Danny and I use to do a lot of rabbit hunting also. His dad, Uncle Ed, tried his best to teach us how to find a rabbit setting and shoot it with a slingshot. We got pretty good with the slingshots, but we never could spot the rabbit setting to shoot it. Uncle Ed would complain about how many bullets we fired and how few rabbits we brought home. One very cold winter day just outside of Campbell Missouri, Danny and I were hunting when we came across a stack of irrigation pipe. We were checking the grass all around the stack of pipes, when we scared up a rabbit and we saw it run into one of the pipe. It was one of the pipe on the bottom of the stack, so, Danny layed down and fired his 22 rifle into the pipe killing the rabbit. Now, that would have been genius, except, now we couldn't get the rabbit out of the pipe. The pipe being on the bottom of the stack, we began unstacking them to get to the one with the rabbit in it. As we got down to the last three levels of pipe, we discovered another rabbit inside. This time I turned the pipe up on one end and the rabbit slid right down into Danny's hands. We were getting really excited now. One pipe had two rabbits in it. That day we took 6 rabbits home and fired one bullet. Uncle Ed enjoyed our story and was happy we had saved our bullets, however, he wasn't too happy to hear we shot a hole in the farmer's irrigation pipe!

Danny and I lived in different counties and we never had the chance to play baseball against each other until our senior year. It was going to be the game of the century. The entire family was going to be there to see us battle. I was a pitcher with a mean curve ball and Dan was a lead off batter, that always hit the first ball. We had teased each other for several weeks about how bad we were going to beat each other. Unfortunately, just before the game was to be played, I went to Florida on our Senior trip and was unable to play against Danny. I know he has always wondered about that game, but, I am sure I would have struck him out…

O Son of mine…

I was raised in the Bootheel of Missouri and like most, I couldn't wait to get away from there. Away from the Cotton and bean fields, the small town with nothing but a grocery store and a small department store which were owned by the same people, the Andersons. It had a saw mill/Box plant that was on its last leg and could no longer support the 1,411 people that lived there. There was no future for me there that I could see. I was no farmer and we had no vehicle to drive somewhere else to work.

Don't get me wrong. I had many life-long friends there that I started to kindergarten and graduated from high school with. I just had to go. So I graduated from high school on a Friday night in June of 1968 and woke up Saturday morning in Dennison Texas, and I haven't looked back since. I will admit that sometimes I yearn for that little town and all that it offered me growing up like the safety and security of everyone watching out for each other and of the kids in town. That is exactly the kind of place I wanted my son to grow up in when I had one.

In 1972 my wish was granted. My wife, Colette gave me a son, Jeffrey Lynn Weldon. I didn't want to scar him with "Terry the second", or "Junior" so I thought giving him my middle name would be safe, so we did. It must have been ok with him, he named his son Blake Lynn. If you are a grandpa, you know what that feels like!

This is what most men dream of, a son, a life-long friend, someone that will always be there for you. Jeff was born on 11 July 1972 in Alton Illinois while I was working at The Montgomery Ward Service Center making somewhere around $75.00 per week. Our mortgage payment was $100 per month so you can imagine how much partying went on at our house. I knew I couldn't continue to support a family of three on that pay so I took and offer to move to Atlanta Georgia and run a Shell Car Care Center. He doubled my pay and off we went. Jeff was not quite crawling so he didn't much care where he went.

We tried Atlanta for about a year and then we headed back toward Missouri. We stopped in Memphis where our cousin Sue and her husband David lived. I went to work at a brand new Goodyear store and this is where I thought I would raise our son.

I grew up in the racially charged 1960s although I had never encountered any situations having to deal with race… until then. I was the service manager for the automotive department of a Goodyear store while another gentleman managed the appliance center and was the overall store manager. He was an outspoken young man who had been raised across the river in West Memphis Arkansas. He had some pretty strong views on integration/segregation. Looking back, I am pretty sure he had a pillow case with two eye holes cut in it somewhere in his home. There was a young black man about eighteen years old came in and applied for a job in the automotive department of the store. I interviewed him and was very impressed. He even changed a couple of tires and the oil in one car to demonstrate his abilities to me. Needless to say the store manager was immediately opposed to the hiring of this young man. He said there were many white guys that needed a job before we hire the likes of this guy. I disagreed and hired him anyway. I decided race had nothing to do with capabilities. Even though we worked together really well for the next six months, this poor guy could do nothing right in the eyes of the store manager. He would criticize everything he did to try and get him to quit, but he wouldn't and I came to respected his steadfastness. One day while I was at lunch the store manager found something to fire him over and did so while I was out. He had made him take his tools and leave. When I returned to the shop and heard what had happened I did something I thought I would never do. I backed my car into the bay, loaded all of my tools and drove off leaving them with no one to work in the automotive department. I went straight down to the recruiter and joined the Air Force. I have often wondered what happened to that young man and how the store manager explained an empty automotive department. But, guys like that store manager seem to get by with that kind of behavior.

Having joined the USAF on a delayed enlistment date, we packed up and moved back to Colette's mom's house for her and Jeff to stay while I was going through basic training. Also, we had our first daughter, Amy, five days after I arrived at basic training. We moved from Biloxi, MS to

Rantoul, IL for more Air Force training. This was a great time to have a son when he is your shadow and had more questions than you had answers. This was the time when I made him eat everything. He would sit at the supper table for two hours before he would eat the food on his plate, then when it was bedtime and we were putting him to bed, we would make him spit out the meat he had for supper and was holding it under his tongue to keep from swallowing it.

I was like most dads and was irritated by all of the questions he could come up with. He wouldn't stop talking. Then I was sent to England for my first assignment in the USAF. I never knew I could miss someone like I did my wife and kids. I would send cassette tapes to them so they wouldn't forget what I sounded like. They sent me tapes also, but Jeff wasn't old enough to figure out what was going on. He kept asking his mom, "Why ain't he talking". I still listen to that tape when I get a chance just to remember him when he was that age.

We came back from England with a son and two daughters Marsha was born while we were over there. We were transferred to Nellis AFB, NV. We tried to make up for all of the things we felt the kids missed while overseas so I started Jeff out in Tee Ball. Of course being the father that knows better than anyone how to teach my son, I began coaching. I tried to be fair and not be harder or easier on my son than anyone else. My advice to fathers in that position is don't coach, just enjoy your son's sport from the bleachers, not in his face. I focused hard on everything except my son, I feel like I missed a lot of the good stuff. I did the same thing with Soccer and the Cub/Boy Scouts. Although we were together most of the time I believe our relationship suffered a little.

As Jeff grew into his teen years I had burned him out on sports. He had no desire to play any longer. He was on his bicycle with his friends and I was TDY for the Air Force most of the time. He was always at the airport to meet me when I returned from a trip, but I think that was because they knew I expected them to be there and not because they really wanted to.

The one thing he excelled in was the ROTC. He was in High School ROTC for five years and rose to the rank of Colonel as the Commandant. I can only remember being at one or two of his ROTC functions during all that time. I hated that part.

Graduation came and Jeff went immediately out into the work force. After a couple of years of working he met and married a girl from Blytheville Arkansas. They relocated to Panama City Florida with the family when I was transferred there in the Air Force. Him and his new bride lived with Colette and the girls while I took a one year side trip to Osan, Korea. Upon my return they moved out and into an apartment. After a few months they decided to return to Arkansas. This was the lowest point in my relationship with my son. I knew at that point I had lost him. That he would not be living down the block from us and spending weekends together fishing and enjoying each other's company. Tough time for me.

I retired from the Air Force and moved to Navarre Florida for a couple of years. Jeff and his family visited us a couple of times while we were there. When Colette and I moved back out to Las Vegas thinking we would enjoy it as a couple of empty nesters, but we were wrong. After one year we returned to Memphis TN. We stayed with Jeff and his new family for a month or so while I settled into my new job. That is when I got to spend a little time with my Grandson, Blake Lynn Weldon. I was sure we would recover some of the time lost over the last few years. Unfortunately for us and fortunately for them, he landed a job just West of St Louis, MO. Again, I had lost him. Too many miles between us to have those fishing trips and weekends together.

I found a job in Flight Simulators and returned to what I had done my entire military career. This quickly moved us all around the South for the next 7 or 8 years. Jeff and his family visited us a couple of times in those 8 years. It was just not the way I first envisioned it.

We have spent a few Christmas' at their house and stop in there when we can and we try to stay in touch, but the phone calls and text messages are getting shorter.

Some time I plan a fishing trip in my head, but we can't seem to get together. The kids were always busy in their activities and he couldn't get away. I keep thinking someday we will find the time.

He surprised us a couple of months ago and came and spent a three day weekend with us. It was great to be with him even if it were just three days.

I am now almost 65 and Jeff is almost 43. We talk on the phone and we text each other sometimes but, there are times when I don't know what to say. I know the love is there but sometimes the words aren't. I love my wife and my girls but, I sure hate it because I lost the relationship with my son that I desperately wanted.

Sometimes it just doesn't work out…

Pass the Pig Skin…

Growing up in Gideon Missouri, there wasn't a great deal to do if it wasn't cotton season. Our school was so small, that if you wanted to join any activity, you could because there weren't enough kids to go around.

I loved baseball and played it all the time, even at home alone by grabbing a stick and batting rock, which I was very good at. I like basketball, but never could figure out why they put the basket fifteen feet up a pole! Well it seemed like it was that tall to me at four feet tall. I played basketball until everyone else out grew me, except Chris Elam, who kept playing anyway.

My cousin, Wayman Baker, who by the way was a grown man at twelve years old was a natural. Of course all he had to do was run over the other team and knock them out of the way. This was easy for him. He enjoyed it so much he wanted me to enjoy it as much as he did and felt for some reason I was missing out on one of life's great pleasures. Every year he would beg me to go out for the team and I would come up with some lame reason why I couldn't until one year I had no good reason. He was so excited for me he could hardly stand it. The first day of practice came and he finally had me psyched. We ran some laps, through the ball a while and ran some laps. We did some sprints and ran some laps. I had been to football games before and other than watching the cheerleaders, I never noticed that much running! Finally we were going to scrimmage. Let's look at the word scrimmage for a second. According to Wikipedia a scrimmage game has "no competitive value of any significant kind to any competitor". If that were the case, why was my own team, guys I grew up with, lifelong friends trying to kill each other? Finally the coach decided to test my skills. I had been watching Chris Elam, who was smaller than me, and he was too small for the other guys to get their hands on him, and he was quick. I thought to myself; I can do that, so in I went. Cousin Wayman was on the side lines as proud as a new Papa. He was coaching me more than the coach was. After a couple of plays, the ball was handed off to me and off I went, straight up the middle, untouched for about thirty yards. I don't remember who hit me; all I remember was not having any air cycling in and out of my lungs like it should have been, just out! I took it like a man and hoped I could breathe again before I got back into formation. I was lucky. I breathed in just as the ball was snapped and for some reason, they gave it to me again. I chose not to go up the middle again, it seemed crowded. I faked to the left, rolled right and off I went. I could actually see the goal line in a distance, just before Ronnie Lowery came in from the left and Kent Reynolds came in from the right. At that point I lost sight of the goal line. Actually, I lost all of my sight for a few seconds! I came to thinking; well at least I didn't get the wind knocked out of me again. I was hoping my eyes would uncross before I got back in formation, and they nearly did when the ball was snapped, and yep, the next thing I felt was the quarterback jamming it into my stomach. Looking out front of me, deciding which direction to go, I remember wondering when the other team added six more players and why they looked like five sets of twins. I heard James Pickard yell at me, "Follow me". Not knowing which one was James; I chose the big guy and fell in behind him. We were off! He was clearing the field in front of me and I was very glad my eyes became clear. Just before the goal line James rolled off to the left to block someone and there he was, Cousin Wayman Baker, six feet,

220lbs, full speed, toward me. I had no place to go but straight ahead, so I lowered my head and was sure I could slip right between his legs. I was wrong. As I came to, I heard Jackie Tolbert say, "I ain't never seen a helmet split down the middle like that". That was my first and last football practice. I don't even watch it on TV…

Pigeon Droppings...

Growing up in and around Gideon Missouri in the 1960s, there wasn't a great deal of entertainment. Our black and white television set got one channel out of Paducah, KY and when the planets were aligned just right we could get a channel out of Memphis, TN.

Like I said, there wasn't a lot to do, so my uncle Smokey Beasley and my brother Jack (Puncho) Weldon raised pigeons. Like that was a huge feat. There were pigeons in every barn in Missouri. However, their goal was to cross breed them until they got all different colored ones.

Uncle Smokey joined the Air Force and my brother moved off to California leaving me with the pigeon crop. Actually, the pigeons lived in the barn and all I had to do was look around the other farms and find different colored squabs, (baby pigeons). Once I found then, I would move a few of them into the nests in our barn. They would grow up with my birds and their babies would be all different colors. It wasn't rocket science.

 A few years after my brother left home he decided to move back to Missouri. He moved his family to Malden one summer and a friend of his from California came with them. His name was "Big Eddie". Typical 1960s Californian, long hair with pony tail, dark tan, tattoos everywhere, kinda little most of the girls of today!

Big Eddie had never heard of catching pigeons before, so he was in for a treat. Me, my brother Puncho, my cousin, Wayman Baker, and Big Eddie took off one hot Summer night to catch us a few pigeons. Wayman knew of an old abandoned barn out in the country where he had seen a few pigeons nesting. We waited until dark and we parked at the road's edge and sneaked across the field to the barn. Now this barn was abandoned for a reason. It was a "leaner" and it could have fell over any minute. I was about 4'11" and about 125 lbs, so I could skinny up the wall of that barn with no problem. Wayman was about 5'11" and about 225 lbs, therefore he didn't skinny to well and he made the old barn creak a little when he climbed the walls. Big Eddie on the other hand was about 6'2" and about 300 lbs. He actually made me a little nervous when he decided he was ready to climb to the rafters and get some pigeons out of the nests.

It was August, not wind moving, and one hundred years of dust in that old barn. The stalls and cribs had been removed and there was only the side walls and a few poles holding the roof up. Nothing but a shell all leaning in one direction, but we had climbed lots of these type structures and didn't have enough sense to be afraid.

I was the first to climb and Eddie held the flash light for me. I took it slow and easy as if I were making a Youtube video on how to steal pigeons! I got to the first nest and very gently, without startling the momma bird, reached in the nest and pulled out the squab, placed it in the burlap bag and climbed on over to the next nest. If you startle the adult pigeons, they will fly straight for the flashlight and I didn't want to freak out Big Eddie… yet!

I had gotten about four squabs in the bag and decided it was time to have a little fun. While I was moving from nest to nest, I had been easing all of the adult birds along the rafter to the corner of the barn. Now it was time to "Let'er Rip". I scared all of the adult birds into flying. They headed straight for Big Eddie and his flashlight! Puncho and Wayman knew what I was doing and turned their flashlights off ensuring Eddie would get the "Full effect". Now, I don't care how large you are and how mean you think you are, when your head is being covered with flapping birds in the dark, you will scream like a little girl the first time; and he did. Once the dust settled and Eddie decided they weren't going to flog him to death, the laughter began.

Eddie couldn't wait for his turn at climbing, so up the side of the barn he started. I could hear the lumber creaking as he worked his way to the top. He was much larger than me and had go a little slower to hang on the edges of those boards. Once he got a little too excited, slipped and down he came, landing in six inches of powdery dust. He had his shirt off, in August. When he landed on the ground flat of his back, he was covered in dust and sweat. He was having the time of his life.

I was on the ground holding the flashlight for Big Eddie, looking up with my mouth wide open when he scared a couple of adult birds down toward me. One was so excited when it flew over my head, it had to "go", I can still taste it everytime I think about that night...

Rabbit Boxes...

Growing up on a small farm was tough in the 1950s and 1960s. Especially if you were a family of sharecroppers. We owned only the things in the house we lived in. Ours was a small wood framed farm house. I don't think we paid any rent, just the utilities. I remember we had a pump house and an outhouse so our water and sewer was free. The electricity was $3.00 per month in 1960s because I can remember seeing the electric bill. We didn't own a vehicle and we had coal heat. I think a load of coal was $50.00 which lasted most of the winter. If we ran low or out of coal, my Granny Beasley had dozens of quilts to pile on if we needed them.

My Uncle Jerry "Smokey" Beasley and my brother Jack "Puncho" Weldon had built several rabbit boxes they used to trap rabbits for our dinner table and some they could sell in town for a little pocket money. After they both left home I inherited their rabbit boxes and added a few of my on. I think I had about twenty total. They were located all around the edge of the fields behind our house as well as along the railroad tracks and in the fence rows around the farm. For those of you who do not know what a rabbit box is, please see the attached photo. It was made of wood, and designed to be placed in the path the rabbit takes on a regular basis, "rabbit run". When the rabbit entered the box, it bumped a trigger which dropped the door behind it and they were trapped inside the box until I made my rounds.

Summer rabbits had lots of warts and few people wanted to buy them, so Fall and Winter was the best time for the rabbit box business. I usually checked my rabbit boxes after breakfast and before school during the week. There was some mighty cold mornings and my rabbit boxes got closer and closer to the house during the winter.

I was always a little afraid to open that trap door on the front of the box and reach my hand in there, not knowing whether or not I had caught a rabbit or a possum. I drilled a hole in the side so I could see what was in there and even then possum hair fooled me. Believe me you will have a completely new outlook on life when you reach for what you thought was going to be a soft cottontail and instead you grabbed a possum by the "less than soft" tail. Do you let go?, not hardly, for letting go gave it a chance to turn around and redesign your hand like a meat grinder. No, you very quickly snatched it out and slung it as far as you could in one fell swoop. I can only remember doing that one time, and I haven't forgotten it.

When the rabbits were in season and healthy enough to eat, I made a few dollars by selling them in town. I had a few regular customers that would buy one any time I brought it by their house. I got $1.00 for a dressed rabbit and .50 cents for an undressed one. That has always sound strange to me because a "dressed" rabbit actually had no skin at all, while an "undressed" rabbit had all of its fur. Every one paid without hesitation except for an old black couple who lived in a little shack of a house on the bank of three ditch. Their names were Joe and Lou Brown. Joe did odd jobs around town while Lou must have raised half the children in Gideon in the 1950s and 1960s. I would always stop by their house on my way back home and give them a rabbit or two. They were always excited to see me and acted like I was giving them a 20 pound ham. You couldn't charge someone who was that appreciative.

I quit messing with my rabbit boxes around 1966 after finding a job in town, but, I will always remember those cold mornings when I had to run my rabbit boxes. I wonder if there are many kids that would do that today to make a little money. Different Generations, Different Ideas…

Raising Grandkids…

  My name is Terry Weldon and I grew up in Gideon Missouri. I lived there from the time I was born in 1950 til the day after high school graduation in 1968. Looking back it was such a short period of time, however, it made the biggest impression on my life than any of the next 45 years since then. I have always heard about the "Good Ole Days", but I never could pin them down. I have enjoyed my life thus far, joining the U.S. Air Force, getting married, having three kids and watching them grow up. But, we usually refer to our childhood years as the good ole days. I think it was because there was something about the unknown. We didn't know what to expect around every corner and that was the adrenalin rush we enjoyed when we were young. It might have been because we were the smartest during our childhood years. I remember when I was a child, like most, I was smarter than the average bear. There was very little I didn't know. When I hit my teen years, I was near-genuis. You couldn't tell me a thing that I didn't know already. I married at the age of twenty and my new bride thought I hung the moon. I could do no wrong. Going into my twenties with children being born, I had a few years of just knowing almost everything again. Once the children began to ask questions, I again was a genius, or at least they thought I was. My thirtysomething years, when the kids were becoming teenagers, I starting going down hill. I mean I was pretty stupid there for a few years. The kids began graduating and leaving home at which time my IQ creeped upward a few points. That was kind of a tough few years with the kids at home thinking you were a total idiot and the ones away from home thought you might have half a brain. Finally, all the kids had graduated and left home, the nest was empty and I was not smart any longer, I was now "Wiser". Just when I thought I had it all back and could focus on my retirement years as a "Wise old man", my wife's view of me had change somewhat over the past forty years. I again, was an idiot! How did all of this happen? I have no idea and am no longer smart enough to figure it out.

The moss it always greener…

One summer my Uncles Ed and Leon Beasley had the rare opportunity to take their families camping together to Reelfoot lake in Tennessee. One last campout before school was starting back. All eight of the kids were there playing all over the campground. They were excited to camp together, but not so happy about returning to school bright and early Monday morning. The three older girls, Jackie, Sue, and Pam were all dressed up like cowgirls and was putting on a wild west show for everyone in the campground. They had no problem being the center of attention! Because the jon boat Uncle Edd had was too small for three, Danny and Ronald were unable to go fishing with the men. Instead, had to stay back and either fish on the bank or play with the girls. Well the girls didn't want that because Danny was somewhat of a perfectionist and everything had to be done his way. Can't imagine where he got that trait.

The girls had been out with Aunt Pauline earlier that morning learning about all of the things you can pick and NOT pick. This is OK, but this will make you itch, this isn't a real berry, we use it as red ink to put our names on our cotton sacks, and this is poisonous DO NOT eat it. They weren't quite as hyperactive as Danny, so they actually paid attention to what was being said. Dan was much happier chasing bugs with a stick or throwing rocks into the lake. He loved to fish, but if he hadn't gotten a bite in ten or fifteen minutes from the dock, he was ready to move on to something else. He also loved talking Ronald into doing anything he could think of. He talked him into climbing a pine tree one time. Ronald shimmied right up that tree to the first limb which was about fifteen feet off of the ground only to discover he could not climb down. Ronald sat on that limb for two hours until Uncle Leon came in from fishing rather than telling his momma what they had done. Uncle Leon got him down and gave them both a spanking. When Uncle Edd came in and found out Dan had gotten a spanking, he gave him another one! However, Dan had a tough behind, and he was usually right back at it in ten or fifteen minutes.

As I said the girls were out herding cattle or roping stumps or something of the sort down by a clump of trees when Danny showed up with his sidekick Ronald. They all yelled and squealed and told them to go away. This just made Danny worse because he had some pretty good ideas when it came to steer wrestling and such. All he needed was a chance to prove himself. The girls weren't having any part of his ideas and managed to run him off, keeping Ronald as a roping steer along with Emily and Linda Carol. Danny was a little upset that the girls wouldn't even listen to his great ideas. As he ran off, he grabbed one of the ropes and threw it around a few cattails growing at the edge of the lake. In his excitement he broke about three or four of them and took off running. The owner of the campground thought the girls did it, took them to their moms and they all got in trouble. Well, if there is one thing the Beasleys can do, that is "hold a grudge" and the girls vowed to get him back for getting them in trouble.

Sunday morning, the last day to enjoy the camping trip, the men had left early to get a jump on the crappie and maybe a few bass. Again, the boys were unable to go so they fished around the dock for a while. Ronald grew bored after a few minutes and went back to see if the girls were up yet. He thought maybe he could try his hand at being a calf again!

Danny wasn't giving up so easy today because he was fishing on top of a boat ramp made of what looked like a giant wooden pallet and he could hear something moving around underneath it. He decided to give that hook a triple dose of worms and slip it down through the crack in the boards. There was such a gob of worms on it, he had to press them through the crack with his fingers. He let the worms drop to the bottom and reeled it up about two turns, when it hit his bait and they were off to the races. Underneath the ramp were lots of cypress stumps for the bass to hide in, and this bass decided to wrap Danny's line around every one of them. All of a sudden hyperactive Danny had the patience of Job. He carefully moved his pole around through that crack until he freed his line and Mr Bass was caught! He reeled him to the top and discovered there was no way to get a three pound bass through a half inch crack. It was about eleven thirty in the morning and Danny had sat there with the fish reeled to the top of the water underneath the boat ramp for about an hour, like some miracle was going to happen. About that time Uncles Edd and Leon came in to grab a sandwich and put the fifty crappie they had caught in the freezer. Danny was yelling for them to come over and see what he had caught. By this time Dannys bass had grown from three pounds to about eight pounds. Yes, he was a true fisherman! Edd and Leon walked over to see this big bass. Edd squatted down and looked through the crack, looked at Danny and praised him for his trophy catch, he then reached into his pocket, pulled out his pocket knife, cut the line and said, "Let's go get something to eat!" Danny thought the sun rose and set in his dad, up to this point. At least for the rest of that day he didn't quite feel that way about him.

After lunch the men had returned to catch some bass of their own and the cowgirls were back riding the range. Ronald was perfecting his role as a roping calf while Emily and Linda Carol opted to stay at the campsite and do almost anything but be a calf! Down by the clump of trees the Jackie, Sue, and Pam had rope burns on just about every part of Ronald's body. At one point they had a rope around one arm, one leg, and his neck. Danny had tried to revive his relationship with the bass under the boat ramp, but wasn't having any luck, He saw that the girls were short on calves to rope and thought he might get in on it. However, his idea was to have Pam be the calf and he be the cowboy. That didn't go over well at all and they soon ran him out of the roping area. He sat down at the base of one of the trees and pouted for a few minutes until he spotted a swarm of honey bees covering a large hole where a tree limb had broken off. Instantly Danny thought, "this is going to be fun" as he jumped to his feet and began gathering rocks from the ground. He chunked a couple of rocks at the honey bees but he couldn't get them to budge. A few of them would fly out a few feet from the rest but returned to join them just as quickly. The girls were in the middle of an all out rodeo and Ronald was almost roped to the ground so none of them were paying any attention to what Danny was up to. In his frustration he picked up a tree limb from the ground and whacked the tree as hard as he could. Well, unknowingly, that did the trick. About a third of those bees headed for whatever made that noise which happened to be Danny. This did get the girls attention and they all three scattered in three different directions, all except Ronald who lay hog tied on the ground with no chance of escape. Danny got frightened and ran to untie Ronald. The bees now "all in a buzz" continued their way to Danny. He knew he couldn't get Ronald untied quick enough, so he just grabbed a rope and began dragging him to safety. All of the bees but five or six headed back to the tree. One of the bees made it to Danny and a couple stopped to visit Ronald. Danny got one sting and Ronald got three or four. Ronald began screaming which put Danny into a panic. The girls saw what happened and ran to his rescue. They all untied Ronald and began treating his stings. Jackie, Sue and Danny began looking around for anything that might help treat him, while Pam headed to the camper to look. While the others were out looking for old Indian remedies, Pam came back with medicine from the first aid kit for bee stings. She rubbed it on him and it almost immediately began to feel better. Jackie and Sue had Danny in a total panic when Jackie had remember with Aunt Pauline had said earlier about a plant that you chewed into a paste that would cure just about anything, but she couldn't remember what it was. Jackie, Sue and Danny argued over what would work on a bee sting when Danny, (who hadn't paid a bit of attention to what Aunt Pauline said) swore it was the moss on the trees. The girls agreed and with that Danny pulled off a hand full and began to chew. By the time they got back to Ronald Danny had it chewed into a nice gob of paste which he spit out and began to rub on the sting bites. They all began to laugh but Danny.

Summer vacation was over and the kids were all decked out in their new school clothes. As they waited for the doors to open to the school Danny was again the center of attention with his bright GREEN lips and gums and teeth and tongue from chewing the moss from the tree which turned out to be the best green dye they ever seen and it lasted for about two weeks...

The Sleigh Ride...

It seemed like the Missouri winters were much worse back in the sixties, much colder and when it snowed, it would stay on the ground for four or five days. When this happened, about the second day of packed snow it was a little too risky for the school buses so we had a day out of school. One of these days I had happened to have spent the night with my cousin Wayman Baker who lived about three miles North of Gideon Missouri in a community known as "Little Walnut" after a grove of walnut trees that stood near the road. Wayman and I were typical young men and we got bored pretty quickly. We had no Gaming systems to pass the time with so we had to use our imaginations. A we were boys and our imaginations were fairly limited.

We were out on their farm pilfering around looking for something to get into. I spotted the perfect thing leaning against the side of the barn, a 1953 Chevy hood. I told Wayman, surely we could come up with something to do with this jewel. A little later we were climbing around in the barn loft and wrestling in the hay. Wayman was about fifteen years old, five feet eleven, 220 lbs. Let's say his seat at the dining table was never empty. In pretending to climb mount everest, or swim across the nile river full of piranha, it came to us like a bolt of lightening. We removed the twenty feet piece of rope from the barn loft, added an eye bolt to the front of the Chevy hood and tied the rop to it. Flipping the hood upside down, it made the perfect snow sled.We pulled it down to the ditch bank, both of us jumped in it and headed down the slope right onto the frozen ditch. We were immediately transformed into the world's best two man bob sled team. Our imaginations were showing improvement. After two or three rides down the ditch bank and pulling it back up to the top, we decided it was too much for two boys, so we drug it back to the barn. Wayman, being the genius he was, came up with a brilliant idea. Lets hook the hood to the rear of the tractor. Do you see how the mind of a fifteen year old genius works? We tied the rope securely to the drawbar of the tractor, Wayman climbed up onto the seat and I jumped into the hood and down the field road we headed. After a couple of trips up and down the field road, we switched off and he rode in the hood and I drove the tractor.I go a little bored just driving up and down the field road and decided to take off across the field. The ground was frozen covered with about a foot of snow. I was right this was a lot funner! Nearing the ditch bank, I made a hard left turn to head down the ridge of the ditch bank. When I did the hood came around and passed me. This was my first lesson in centrifugal forces.I learned pretty fast with a thirty foot rope starting to wrap around the front of the tractor. Being young and having quick reactions, I hit the brakes of the tractor before I damaged the hood. Once my laughter subsided, I also quickly noticed, Wayman was no longer in the hood! I shut off the tractor and ran over to the crest of the bank. There he was in the fetal position on the far side of the ditch underneath some brush, not moving. Oh my God, I thought, I have killed him! He had on a pair of his dad's insulated coveralls and was looking like a tan polar bear. I thought, how will I explain this to Uncle Hob and Aunt Peg. As I was compiling my story in my head, he rolled over with tears running down his cheeks from laughter. He crawled up the ditch bank and said "Let's do that again".

I decided I had gotten my blood pressure high enough for a guy my age, so we went back to the house and had a couple of bologna sandwiches and a tall glass of milk, each. W were excited about the new game we had came up with and we were anxious to show someone. We filled up the tractor and headed into Gideon, three miles away. The rods were snow packed and the road ditches were filled so the hood would float along behind the tractor. Coming across three ditch bridge on the North end of Gideon we turned left down North Walker Ave stopping and picking up Ronnie Lowery. We then turned right on E Railroad St, then left on N Gideon Ave. As we passed Roy Elam's store Kent Reynolds hopped on with us and we continued on. When we corner by Davis' Groceries, Shelby Wingo tossed me his crutches and jumped on board as we turned left and crossed to road, Vickie and Toby Jordan hopped aboard and we were pretty much at our limit. We knew a great place to ride and be out of the traffic, the ballpark across the highway from my house. We crossed three ditch headed East for about a quarter of a mile. We turned right and headed down the snow covered gravel road and onto the ball field, covered in freshly fallen snow. It was snowing at the time and that made it perfect for a sleigh ride. As we pulled to hood all around the ball park, slinging guys off into the outfield fence and laughter away the pain, a police car came driving up and called us over. No one told us what we were doing was illegal...

Them Bones…

I just read another great story by Jim Ferguson about his and Chris Elam's adventures as Indian relic finders. There were lots of Indian mounds in our part of the country. Almost everyone I knew had an Indian arrow head collection, but only these two guys could claim they found the skeleton of an Indian.

I remember the news of their find was all over the bootheel of Missouri. At that point, everyone in school was their best friends. You know how it is with celebrities! Like most stories, it lasted a couple of weeks and we no longer knew "ole' what's his name and his sidekick". There was some story about them shipping the skeleton to St Louis or some university up north to have it checked out by some hornatholigist, or kinagoligist, or one of those bone geniuses to verify it's validity.

One weekend, me, Kent Reynolds, Loren Stephens, and Vick Jordan were out at my house trying to find something to do. We wondered over to the ballpark and looked for foul balls in the thorn bushes. It was very dark and the foul balls were in the thorn bushes, so that didn't last very long, once we all were bleeding from the thorns.

We ventured on over to the old airport building to have a look around. I had lived there all of my life and had never seen inside of it. It was no longer used for anything and we weren't planning on damaging it, so we thought that would be OK. It was one of those cloudy nights where the clouds were moving and the moonlight would only come through occasionally. As we neared the building, as boys do, we started telling creepy tales to frighten one another. I will be the first to admit, you didn't have to tell me a very creepy story to scare me. I am pretty sure my friends were the same way, they just wouldn't admit it. The closer to the building we got, the darker it was and the quieter we all were. The door was locked, so we split up and began looking for an unlocked window, Kent and I went together and Loren and Vick went the other direction. Kent and I found a window unlocked and crawled inside to take a peek. It was very, very dark. I think if we had not been somewhere around fifteen years old, we might have been holding hands! Once inside it was dead silence, all we could hear was Loren and Vick still trying to find a way in, then we heard the screech of a window being opened and again, nothing. We were both sort of giggling, nervously, as we eased around the wall in the dark. Finally we walked straight into the other two guys and we all had a pretty good scare from that. Then it began to be more funny than scary. I told them I had seen people from my house walking around on top of the building, like it had an observation deck on top. We all started sliding our hands down the wall trying to find a door that might lead upstairs. One of us found it and the others eased back along the wall, trying to step when the moonlight was showing the waybecause we had no idea what might be stored in that room. Eventually we all made it to the top and enjoyed a breath of fresh air. We jumped around and acted like a bunch of six year olds. It was a hot summer night and it wasn't long before the sweat began to pour from our foreheads. It was time for a break, we sat down to cool down and someone started with the scary stories again. We had each other pretty frightened when we saw car lights turn off of the highway and head down the gravel road toward us. We all sat down behind the walls of the observation deck where no one could see us and waited to see what the car was going to do. It was a pickup truck and it drove just past the building we were in and out of sight of the highway. It was a couple coming out here to "Park", and it was my old friend Dennis Skidmore. The girl shall remain nameless! Once we saw who it was we decided, this was going to be the best "scare" of the year. He had no idea there was anyone else around. Ladies and gentlemen, this was going to be epic! We sat on top of the building and planned every detail of how we were going to scare Dennis and his date.

Once we decided what we were going to do, we began to work our way down stairs. We were all huddled together and stepping on each other's feet, snickering and giggling like school girls. Once we were at the bottom of the stairs we huddled for one last plan of attack. The best way to get out was through the window Kent and I had entered through, so we decided to just cut straight across the room and out the window. Still in sort of a huddle we all started across the room. Creeping slowly and waiting for the moonlight to light our way, however, we got too excited and all started to run across together. After about three or four steps, it was there in front of us, about three feet wide and six feet long and about six inches off of the floor. It was too late, we all were wadded together and had too much momentum to stop and down we all went. I, of course was on the bottom. Vick Jordan came down on top of me and I felt my face mash into what appeared to be dirt, at least it tasted like dirt. At that exact moment, the clouds parted and the moonlight came shining in. What we didn't know was they had placed the Indian skeleton in a crate filled with dirt and left it there to be flown to St Louis. As I turned my head sideways to spit out some dirt, my nose was touching the skull of that Savage Warrior! First we said it; then we did it!

We flew by his truck, all of us trying to wipe that creepy dead Indian off of us. I'm not sure Dennis ever knew we were even out there that night…

The Pump House...

We lived about a half mile outside of town; therefore, we didn't have "city" water. Instead we had a well in the back yard. Once the well was drilled, instead of a pump handle on top, we had an electric motor and pump. The pump had a small five or ten gallon tank on it so it wouldn't lose its prime I think. The problem with this configuration was it would freeze in the winter and burst the tank or the lines. To prevent this from happening, my Grandpa P.O. built a "pump house" around it. It was about four feet by four feet square and stood about three feet tall. In order to service the motor and pump, Grandpa put a removable roof over it and sort of sloped it so the rain would run off of it.

Our pump house sat out back under the tree about twenty five feet from the back porch. To keep this structure from being "unsightly" from the travelers going down the highway at seventy miles per hour, Grandpa put shingles on it to match the roof of our house. That would be ok, but he also shingled the sides to help insulate it from the cold weather. Inside the pump house was packed with insulation also keeping the cold out.

One summer night when I was about fourteen or fifteen years old, I had returned home from a evening out with my friends. It was a warm summer night so I raised my bedroom window next to my bed and lay with my head almost on the window seal enjoying the cool night air. As I was about to drift off to dreamland, my eyelids began to flicker. At first I thought it was lightening from a distant thunderstorm out of hearing range. I batted my eyes a couple of times to clear them and hoped I didn't have glaucoma at fifteen years of age. However, just before dosing off they began to flicker again. I opened them and stuck my head out the window, which was very easy, with no screen in it, to get a better look outside. The pump house was just out of my view until I turned and looked further into the back yard. To might surprise, the pump house was on fire and really starting to burn, but good! I jumped from my bed and ran to the front of the house where Granny and Grandpa slept, yelled out, "the pump house is burning, the pump house is burning"! My grandparents hit the floor running, Granny in her sleeping gown and me and Grandpa in our underwear, which I might add, mine looked a lot better than his, and we all headed out the back door to save the pump house. We all three stood there at first evaluating the situation, then Grandpa ran to the edge of the porch to grab the water hose and turn on the faucet, only to discover someone had cut the end of the water hose off for a siphoning hose, which is an entirely different story that we won't get into right now. Once he discovered there was no water available to put out the fire and the tar from the shingles was melting and beginning to drip down the back side of the pump house onto the tree trunk, which would start the tree burning and we would really be in trouble then. Grandpa yelled at me to grab the opposite side of the pump house roof and we could carry it away from the tree to a safer place. With a little reluctance in my voice I asked if we might not want to rethink that idea. In a somewhat different voice, he rephrased his request to where I understood perfectly, so I grabbed hold and we took off away from the tree. Because the tar from the shingles was melting and dripping from the roof, there were several balls of this hot tar across the yard back to the pump house, of which Grandpa stepped on most of them going back to fight the fire. Now here is where me and Forrest Gump had a few things in common, "stupid is as stupid does". When Grandpa's bare feet hit those little balls of hot tar, he began to do this strange dance, unlike anything I had ever saw him do before, actually I didn't know he could dance at all! Now back to me and Forrest Gump, I began to laugh, out loud. Yep, you heard me right, I laughed out loud at something not all of us gathered in the back yard that night thought was funny! I know Grandpa was in severe pain, but I thought I saw the tiniest of grins on my Granny's face that we never talked about, ever! As Grandpa sat on the back porch and peeled the tar balls and most of the skin off the bottom of his feet and the pump house burned to the ground, I thought boy this is going to make a funny story forty years from now!

The Bug…

I was raised from 1954 to 1967 on a farm across the road from the Baseball park just East of Gideon, Missouri. I was four years old when we moved there. My Grandpa, P.O. Beasley was a sharecropper working for Hershell Bell in the 1950s and 1960s. Our house was next to the highway and sat on about an acre of land, depending on how they farmed the land. It seemed like they plowed closer to the house every year.

My Aunt Margie Beasley was still living at home and going to high school at Gideon when she met a young Air Force man stationed at Blytheville AFB, Arkansas in the early 1960s. They were married shortly after they met and she moved to Blytheville where they lived in a small apartment . I would catch the bus at Portageville and for thirty five cents get a ride to Blytheville. A year or so later, they were expecting their first child. That is when they bought a mobile home, moved it into the yard beside our house. Now that Uncle Ben needed to drive from Gideon to Blytheville every day to work he needed some good transportation. This is when they bought the bright shiny blue 1965 Volkswagen Bug. As far as I was concerned, being 15 years old, it was like a new Corvette! All I wanted to do was get behind the wheel and let the wind blow throw my hair. But, first there was a small task of getting a driver's license.

Teaching me to drive was fairly easy for Ben and Margie, it was like breaking a new pony, just take me out into the newly plowed field and "let me run". No ditches to run in to, no traffic to contend with and no trees to "climb". After a few days of that I was ready for the highway. One minor difference in the fields and the road; the road had limits as to how far you could drive to the left or right, ditches as it were. Then some fool painted a line right down the middle of the road. How was I suppose to stay on one side of that, and why the right side? Shouldn't I be on the left side of the road where I could see the road ditch better. Do I care how close I am to the oncoming cars? There was no traffic coming, why couldn't I use the middle of the road? It looked safer to me.

No one mentioned a driver's handbook. This didn't look good at all. I studied for what seemed like months, which I am sure was only weeks before I was ready. Uncle Ben told me not to be too cocky because the written test was tricky, but I was positive I would ace this test, with no problems! Well, I failed it; give signal 100 feet before, don't pass on double yellow lines, parallel parking. I was doing just fine out in that cotton patch without all the dad-blasted rules to hold be back. It wasn't so much the rules, or the instructor treating me like a child, or even me running the stop sign during the driver's test that bothered me. It was the fact that I had to tell my first "car date" that I failed the test and we weren't going to be able to go out. She was devastated I'm sure. That, my friends, was pretty embarrassing stuff for a 16 year old in 1966. Now it was really on. I had seven days before I could test again and I was going to ace it for sure this time; I passed the written test by one question, which, for all of you that don't know, is as good as acing it!

Driver's license in hand and hours of Ford Ferguson driving experience disking turn rows behind me, all I had to do was stay on my Aunt Margie and Uncle Ben's good side so they would let me use their VW Bug and I was in there. I lived with my grandparents growing up and can only remember us having an old GMC pickup truck which we didn't have for long. Either my Grandpa or my Uncle Smokey ran it up one of the rails of an iron-railed bridge and I believe that was the last of our vehicles. If my Granny and Grandpa wanted something, they simply called one of their eleven kids and some thirty grandkids and presto, there it was. Having no vehicle really didn't do a lot for my "social networking life" and we were still forty years away from Facebook! Most of the time, my friends, Dennis Skidmore, Loren Stephens, James Pickard, and Vick Jordan, when he could fight off his brothers, Toby and Tommy Jordan for his parent's car were always willing to give me a lift if I needed it. Also my cousin Wayman Baker made sure I never needed a ride anywhere if he was available, but in 1966, I sometimes needed some "alone with a girl" time if you know what I mean. With all that in mind, it was extremely important for me to do what my "neighbors in the yard" wanted me to do. I soon convinced them I was an excellent baby sitter which was OK for a while. However, they discovered I could baby sit on Friday and Saturday night while they went out on the town. At that point, the baby sitting job kinda back-fired on me.

But to be honest, they would go out one of those nights and give me their car with a full tank of gas on the other night along most Sunday afternoons.

I was kinda cool being the only guy around Gideon with a VW Bug available. Especially, because I could get seven kids in it "comfortably". Well, I was comfortable and all those boys with a girl on their laps never complained!

I tried my best to respect their rules and have the car back home by eleven or so. One night I was dropping someone off over on J highway just West of Malden, MO. I was running a few minutes late and may have been going slightly over the posted speed limit by a couple of miles per hour, when something that looked like a red-haired Big Foot ran out in front of me. I slammed on the brakes but it was too late. It was a very large Red-Bone hound with the biggest head I ever saw. He started with his head just above the handle of the trunk, which was in the front of the car, (caved in the hood). He then rolled over and placed his back just above the windshield onto the roof, (cracked windshield). Rolling one more loop, his big head banged right in the center of the roof, caved it in about three inches. I saw the hound roll off of the top of the car and into the grassy road ditch. I knew he was done for and there was nothing I could do for him so I continued home to try and explain. Uncle Ben and Aunt Margie were still up when I got home at around 11:30pm. I did my show and tell about the biggest Red-Bone hound I had ever seen to Uncle Ben. He rolled his eyes, looked over the amount of damage and found no hair anywhere and decided he wanted to see it for himself. We loaded up and headed back to J Highway. To this day we have never found a trace of any red-bone hounds along that strip of highway. Uncle Ben was a understandably upset, but what about me, I had clearly encountered the first Red-Haired Sasquatch in Southeast Missouri and came out unharmed, what about me!

The Carpenter...

I have written several things about my Grandpa P.O. Beasley and most of them ended up with the smell of alcohol. Although he did like his Colonel Lee whiskey on the weekend, he was a sober, hard working man the rest of the week.

Most all of his family was from Alabama, but for some odd reason he was born in Dekalb County Texas. Never hear the story as to why and he had passed away before I knew this and couldn't ask him. He never really spoke of his family very much. I knew he met my Granny Beasley back in Alabama. They were married and moved to Hazen Arkansas. I saw in the Census tht his dad had remarried and wa also living in Hazen AR but I never knew the story.

As I said he was a hard working man who knew nothing but farming. He was a sharecropper all of my life working for U.S. Holiman and Hershell Bell in and around Gideon, MO.

Because sharecropping is a tough, low paying job, he also did a little carpentry around town to bring in a little extra income. He would repair porches and replace shingles on houses mostly as I was growing up. He taught me how by having me help him on many of the odd jobs. Over time he would find the job, give them a quote and start the work. I would come in and finish it while he worked on the farm. It was his was of teaching me a necessary trade and letting me make a little pocket money too.

He was a strict disiplinarian and what he said was the law. I can't ever remember talking back to him. I didn't always agree with him, but I had a great deal of respect for him.

The Flatbed…

I started school at Gideon Elementary with the same people I graduated with. A few came and went, but for the most it was the same core of classmates throughout my school days.

Each person was a special friend for a different reason. One of those friends later in my school day was Dennis Skidmore. Dennis was a real competitor in everything he did. He was a natural athlete and excelled in all of them. He ran in track and field in school and held several of the athletic records for a while in high school. I, on the other hand was a little small to compete with him, but there was one thing I could do, "set ups". Because of my size and physique I could do set ups until you got tired counting. When we were in high school, I wanted to be on that records board so badly I would have paid the judges. But I didn't. I saw the record board and every other name was Dennis Skidmore. I went after the set ups record, thinking he didn't care much about that one, however, Dennis cared about them all. I took the record for setups; I don't remember how many I did, but it was in the hundreds, his name came down and my name went up. Proud as a peacock, and cocky as one to, I really rubbed it in to Dennis. The very next month, he beat my record. Friends are friends and competitors are competitors, next month I took it back. Coach Brawner really enjoyed this type of competition and he coaxed it on. Coming down to the end of our school year Dennis took it back and there wasn't enough time for me to try again before school was out. I didn't want to leave school without my name on that board, but it wasn't to be. However, I did receive the "PhysEd" award that year. I think it was out of pity, but I didn't care what the reason, Dennis didn't get it!

Just before school was out there was some talk of getting rid of "Senior skip day", of course they would during our Senior year. Dennis Skidmore, Kent Reynolds, Ron Lowery, James Pickard, and myself decided we might be able to influence that decision. One Friday we made sure the science room window was left unlocked, that night we went out and gathered up, possums, turtles, some chickens, and two snakes. We opened the window to the science room and deposited all these critters, making sure the door to the hallway was left open and the game was free to roam. Our thought pattern was they would let school out Monday while they cleared out the school not knowing how many were loose inside, clever uh?. Some more of that Forrest Gump thinking, stupid is as stupid does, and we all actually graduated. Little did we know the Janitors came in sometimes on the weekends. They simply opened the doors and let all of the critters out. Then they stood back Monday morning and looked out for guys that looked like Forrest Gump. I am sure we stood out like a sore thumb. We tied one of the snakes to the chain on the flagpole, (really funny in 1967), but the custodians refused to take it down. Someone, (not me), Dennis I think, snitched on James Pickard and he had to take it down.

Dennis had many girlfriends throughout his high school years, but one stands out in my memory; ole' what's her name. It was her birthday and Dennis wanted to do something special, so he came to me for ideas. He came to the right person, I had a great idea. I had recently seen a wedding where they released these beautiful white doves just before the couple left the church. We didn't have white doves, but I had a barn full of pigeons. Dennis came over that night, we caught ten pigeons, some of which were white, the next day we waited until school was over and everyone was gone, but the doors weren't locked. We sneaked in and placed those pigeons in her locker. Then, the next morning she would open her locker and "SURPRISE". This was a near- brilliant idea if I do say so myself. The next morning Dennis and I parked ourselves just around the corner from ole' what's her names locker and waited for the "Grand Opening". It couldn't have went any better, she opened the locker and out the birds came. The hallway was packed with kids and it might as well been everyone's birthday, because they all got a big surprise. We watched as she stood there in total amazement, she was just staring into her locker and then she started to cry. Something had went wrong with this surprise. Dennis and I ran over to her and what we didn't think about had happened. Those pigeons had crapped all over everything in her locker, ruining her books, tennis shoes and gym clothes. I turned to Dennis and said, "I told you this was a dumb idea".

Dennis' parents always treated me like one of their own

when I went to visit. Dennis had chores to do. If he had done them, we could take their pickup truck out on the weekends. One Friday night there was a special function with two knock-out dates and we sort of had to dress up. I actually don't remember the two girls, but they were foreigners, from way over in Malden, Missouri. For some reason Dennis had not done his chores, I am sure he had a very good reason. When it was time to go, he asked his dad for the truck keys. His dad said, sorry you didn't finish your chores. He said to unload the flatbed truck full of hay bales and stack them under the pole barn. We had backed the flatbed under the pole barn and planned to unload it in the morning, however, his dad had a different idea, namely, do it now! We began tossing that hay for all we were worth. The darker it got, the harder we threw them. We planned to come back and straighten them out the next morning. After telling his dad we were finished, he decided to check our work because we were a little too energetic. He came out, saw bales of hay all over the place and said, sorry boys, no truck. We begged, but he was a little upset with us and told us if we just had to go out that evening, we could take the flatbed, thinking we would be so embarrassed, we wouldn't go. This old rust bucket was held together by Missouri gumbo and baling wire. It hadn't had water on it since we drove it into the road ditch the month before. Being the men that we were, we didn't back down, we jumped in the flatbed and took off. We took these two girls to their homecoming football at Malden where everyone in town could see us. We never saw those two girls again. I told Dennis it was a dumb idea!

The Front Porch...

"Nobody thought much about the front porch when most Americans had them and used them. The great American front porch was just there, open and sociable, an unassigned part of the house that belonged to everyone and no one, a place for family and friends to pass the time."

--Rochlin, *The Front Porch*, in *Home, Sweet Home*

It was an August Saturday evening around five o'clock. Granny Beasley sat in the porch swing fanning herself with the fan she got at the revival last week. It had a flat stick for a handle and a thin cardboard picture of Jesus knocking at a door. I am sure most of you remember those fans. On the other side was an advertisement for fertilizer or some other farm product. She was fanning, swinging very slightly, humming "Rock of Ages" and staring out over the cotton fields. I often wondered what she was thinking, but never asked. I am 63 years old and now I'm sure I think about the very same things. I lay on the porch with my legs hanging over the edge and felt the evening sun hugging me just before it settled behind the small town of Gideon, Missouri. It was the mid 1960s, we had no air conditioning, so the slight breeze blowing across the front porch was all we had and it felt great. I can still remember enjoying those moments in time.

The front porch might be just large enough to set a couple of rocking chairs on it, or it might wrap completely around the house with rocking chairs grouped together on every side for each generation to socialize on. The front porch was an outdoor living room where we gathered after supper. When the house was hot and muggy, we all moved out to the front porch to cool off and wind down after a full day of activities. Aunt Margie would sit in the swing to dry her hair after she had washed it and jump to run into the house every time a car passed, thinking it was a boy coming to see her. If we had family over, the kids would play in the front yard while the adults talked about what has been going on in their lives, express their opinions on world events, or just simply enjoy each others company by saying nothing. I remember the topic for a few years was the Vietnam war because Uncle Ben Termin and Uncle Smokey Beasley were over there and we were all concerned about their safety and well being. God was good and they both made it home safe and sound. There were fifty people standing on that front porch when they returned from the war.

The front porch was both a private and a public domain. It was where intimate family discussion took place one day and all sorts of salesmen tried peddling their goods or services the next day. I watched my grandparents sign up for a family burial plan with Bradshaw funeral home on the front porch while I also watched my grandpa toss a few overbearing salesmen off that same front porch. Many times the neighbors would come by and stop on the front porch to pass the time of day and never enter the house.

It was hard to walk down the street and see families on their front porch without saying "Hello". It was almost mandatory to speak if you made eye contact with someone on their front porch. Because it was a public area, if you were on the front porch, you too, were obligated to speak to the passerby.

The front porch might take on the appearance of the Grand Ole Opry on a Saturday night bursting at the edges with music and dance, then, Sunday morning the only sound you heard was the turning of the pages as Granny Beasley read the family Bible just before church.

My Grandpa P.O. Beasley slept off a few trips to town on Saturday as Granny left him lying there on the front porch, Winter and Summer!

There were lots of houses which were simply "Cracker" boxes until the front porch was built. Once the front porch was completed it took on it's own personality. Some were cold and damp while some were bright and cheery. Some were brightly painted and decorated and there were others that never saw an ounce of paint nor a hanging fern. The personality mostly depended on the people that lived in the house at the time.

The front porch was a major part of American society for many years. Somewhere around WWII this all began to change. The front porches in America began to shrink and disappear. Houses were getting more expensive and money was saved by cutting back on the front porch or cutting it out completely. The Television, air conditioner, and the automobile proved to aid in eliminating the social function of the front porch. The front porch was no longer an important feature to the American people. We went from listening to the radio on the front porch and talking face to face, to eating "TV" dinners in front of the "Boobtube"; and now FACEBOOK. Families no longer relax and social out on the front porch. Family values are no longer established while the children and their parents sat and talked on the front porch.

The question is, "Where are the family values being developed today"?

The Man…

It was the 7th grade, my first year in the high school building and I was somebody now! Loren Stephens, Kent Reynolds, and Vicky Jordan had dared me to run to the back of the boiler to see what was back there. I was no coward nor could I pass up a dare. I eased the door open, listening for some form of life in there then tip toed inside. It was larger than life back then. I would have thought you could heat the entire city of Gideon with that boiler. I continued toward the back to see what mysteries lie in wait for me. Once I got there all I saw was a couple of dust coats and some brooms and mops. Quite a let down at the time. I turned to report back to my crew and there he was, 6 feet 6 inches, 230 pounds, built like a lumber Jack, at least that is the way I saw Vernon Tolbert for the first time. For those of you that know Vernon, I might have been a little off on his size, regardless, he was "The Man" and I had been caught on his turf. Before he could say hello and ask what I needed, I was out of there like a flash, trying to blend into the crowd while heading for my next class.

As the months went by I saw Vernon again as he was sweeping the hallway, every time we made eye contact, he gave me the "evil eye", like he knew it was me that time in the boiler room. He had changed in size somewhat, but he was still "The Man" and I had to stay out of his way or get on good terms with him somehow. By the eighth grade I was an old timer around the high school, I had even talked a few

7th graders into going into the back of the boiler room.

As an eighth grader, we started using the "new gym" for Physical Education (PE). Of course it was known all over the New Madrid and three adjoining counties that NO ONE walked on the gym floor with street shoes, no exceptions.

One day just at the end of PE class, the coach was called to the office which was in the main building. We finished our class and headed for the showers. After our showers we were standing by the bleachers waiting for the bell to ring when one of my "good friends" dared me to try my hand at a free throw because he knew I would never have a chance at a shot from the sidelines. I thought, I could probably make a free throw and I had on my U.S. Keds which were not really street shoes. I strolled out onto the court took a couple of bounces with the ball and with all I had from my 4 foot 6 inch physique away the ball went. I would say it was about five feet from being the best free throw in that gym ever, when who walked around the corner and said "nice shot", Vernon Tolbert! How could this happen twice? At this point he was bigger than I thought. I knew custodians couldn't spank students, but he was still "The Man" and I did push the broom for the next four PE classes.

I did make it to the 9th grade which means you are nobody. No longer Jr high, but not quite high school. We were always looking for some way of getting attention and I was no different than the rest. One beautiful summer day we were all outside for lunch when one of my "good friends" dared me to run up one of the beams of the new gym and over the top and down the beam on the other side. Do you see a pattern here? Yes, I did, and Yes Vernon Tolbert was on the other side waiting for me. This is the time I learned how to wax the floor of the gym!

Sophomore year came and we were somebody again, one of the high school kids finally. Halloween that year was a gloomy night, winter was a little early and it was drizzling rain. Several of us gathered in the parking lot behind the school. Everyone had a couple of rolls of toilet paper. You could throw those things really high and they would trail over those trees perfectly. We had all thrown our rolls and were hurrying to get out of there, as we rounded the corner of the building I found a roll that hadn't been used, I grabbed it and chunked it over the tallest tree when I heard a voice from a dark corner of the building say "Nice throw". You guessed it, Vernon Tolbert! Because he was "The Man", I spent the next day with a water hose washing all of that toilet paper out of those trees.

Junior year I had begun trade school where we went to school at Gideon and caught another bus to school on the Air Base at Malden, then back to Gideon for the afternoon classes. I was excited about this adventure until I got to school and found the bus to trade school and there he was, Vernon Tolbert was the driver. Why was I being punished, I never dated or even hit on any of his daughters, and he had plenty of them. All went well the first couple of months until I got caught smoking on the bus, then I rode in the front seat the rest of the year.

My senior year came and my life changed. My Grandparents, P.O. and Dollie Beasley, who had lived in the same house across the road from the ballpark at Gideon, Missouri since I was one year old, had a house built in Clarkton Missouri. We had no car and I couldn't possibly go to school my senior year at Clarkton. When Vernon Tolbert heard about my problem, he changed the route he drove to trade school and picked me up at Clarkton every morning of my senior year allowing me to finish school where I started, Gideon High, Class of 68'. Vernon Tolbert, you are "The Man".

The Old Barn...

I grew up about a half mile East of Gideon, Missouri. Just across the road from the ball park and the airport. I believe the population was 1,411 when I moved there and 1,412 when I left. For the first 12-14 years of my life, the one square mile around a small farm house was my whole world. I knew every dirt clod by name. We were sharecroppers for Hershel Bell. It was flat farmland that changed top soil every time the wind came up. Summers were hot, mosquitoes were large and baseball was the great American past time.

Winters, on the other hand, were cold and gloomy. Snow came and went pretty regularly and the ice came in November and stayed until March. The winter wind would cut your ear lobes like a ginsu knife. Playing outside was out of the question except for one place; the old barn. The second floor of the barn over the corncrib was full of hay. Some of the most sophisticated tunnels in the world were designed in that old barn. We would build the tunnels during the winter to play in out of the cold weather. When summer came around we had fed the top off of every tunnel to the livestock.

The girls in our family would bring their friends over and play in the hay. We would play hide and seek in the tunnels hoping to steal a kiss from one of the friends. Looking back I wonder how many times I thought I was stealing a kiss from one of the friends in the darkness of those tunnels, and how many times it was actually a cousin I was kissing. That may be where the phrase "Kissing Cousins" came from! It could be 30 degrees outside, but, after 10 minutes of crawling around in those hay tunnels, we were sweating like a pig while our coats hang on an old rusty nail.

Even when there was no one visiting, there was nothing like lying in the hayloft on that soft fresh hay, watching the rays of sunlight come through the cracks between the boards of the wall, seeing every particle of dust gently float by as you lay there taking in the sweet smells of the old barn, and some not so sweet.

That old barn was also home to some of the most beautiful pigeons I ever saw. We called them "our" pigeons, but they were free to come and go as they pleased. They would fly in and out of the barn through the hayloft doors on each end until a tornado came through one summer and removed a few sheets of tin from the roof. After that storm they could come and go much easier through those holes in the roof making it almost impossible to catch them. I am sure I heard them sitting on the rafters laughing at me as I climbed the side of the wall knowing they could wait until I got right to the top and they could be long gone before I could reach them. Wasn't as much fun after that, but they were much happier.

There was no livestock kept in the old barn except the occasional pig my grandpa would raise for ham and bacon, or a goat that ended up as a nice barbeque one Sunday. It held mostly some corn, toad-sacks, baling wire and quite a lot of hay.

Some times as we were moving around the bales of hay one

would "accidently" break open. It was usually those bales that were held together with ROPE instead of baling wire. Today hay bales are bound with nylon string. You might call it baler twine, binder twine, hay rope and various other unmentionable names when it becomes tangled around your feet. When this happened , we had no choice but to add it to the mound of soft hay already in the loft. This was located directed underneath the long rope hanging from the ceiling tied to the main rafter of the barn. I'm not saying this was dangerous, but I have seen, and felt, a rope burn or two resulting from this rope. I am also not sure how many kids this rope would hold, but it was a lot! I often wondered; if they didn't want us playing in the barn loft, why did they put all that soft hay and tie that rope up there?

Also, why on earth would they build those old barns using so many rusty nails? Didn't they ever hear of galvanized nails that don't rust? I can't tell you how many times I have stepped on, raised my head against, or backed into a rusty nail in the barn. The only thing worse than the nails were the splinters! Wasn't there some builder's code back then where they had to sand every board they used to build a barn? There should have been. Most of the splinters were from sliding your hands along the wood as you were climbing around the barn loft and were easily removed through a few tears, however, there were those "special" splinters that would find their way about an inch underneath the nail bed of your fingers. I call them special, because they would stay with you until your finger nail grew out enough to allow you to reach them with some wire cutters, we didn't have any tweezers lying around the barn back then. I can still feel that finger throbbing after the infection set in. There is now other feeling like it. You wanted to rip off the fingernail to pull that rascal out, but you couldn't stand touching it. Seemed like when it was at near peak infection, you would somehow manage to hit it with another piece of wood you were using for a hammer. That is where most of us learned those really good cuss words!

The old barns have stood faithfully out behind the main house in the edge of the field, unpainted with livestock using them as a porta-potty. Those old barns that stored all those treasures and kept all those secrets of what went on inside all those hay lofts. Built as cheaply as possible, yet lasting for a hundred years and more. The beauty of those old barns is that they now are some of the most expensive wood you can buy in the United States. Way to go my old friends…

You can trust me…

Around 1964, of my grandparent's children had all left home except me and my Aunt Margie. My Aunt Margie and I became very close when I was around fourteen years old and up. Although I had one sister already, "Sissie", Margie was as close to a second sister as one can get. We were thick. I covered for her when she wanted to slip away from the house on occasion and she would help me get to stay in town a while longer by calling Granny and telling her I was helping in the beauty shop where she worked.

Margie went to work at the beauty shop when she was about seventeen years old. When she had to work late, I would walk up to town and sweep the beauty shop floor for fifty cents and then I would walk her home.

If you have read any of my other stories, you probably remember how dark it got from three ditch bridge to our house which was about the longest quarter mile in the world, especially if you were scared of the dark to begin with, which "she" was.

One night there was about ten to fifteen people at our house for supper when Margie called to say she was about finished at the beauty shop and would I meet her at the three ditch bridge to walk the rest of the way home with her. Being the loving little "brother" I was, I told her sure, I would be there in twenty minutes.

One of my cousin's (Carmelita Baker), had just married and she and her husband (Bill Smith) were over for supper. I told Bill that I sure knew a way to have some real fun with Margie. After he heard my plan, he agreed. It went something like this; I would meet Margie at the bridge while Bill hid in the road ditch about half way between the bridge and our house, he would wait until we passed him, jump from the ditch and scare the beegeebees out of her. Man that was going to be more fun that you could imagine.

I walked to the bridge and when I got there it was pitch black. Darker than usual, with overcast skies and just a glooming night. Perfect for what we were about to do. She wasn't there when I got there; guess I was early just waiting for the fun to begin. I sat upon the railing of the three ditch bridge in the darkness that was beginning to close in on me. Soon, I heard her coming. I began to get exited again. As soon as she got to me, she grabbed my hand and said, let's get on home, that it was too spooky out that night. Crap, now she's starting to scare me. Being the man I was at fourteen, I told her to take it easy, I wouldn't let anything happen to her, hehe.

Because it was so dark that night and of course, there was no traffic to see the road from their headlights, we walked as close to the middle of the road as we could. When we came close to where I thought Bill was hiding on the left side of the road, I tried to ease us over toward him to make this even better. We walked another fifty feet and, no Bill. I thought he had gotten tired waiting on us and went on back to the house, so I moved back to the middle of the road, when it happened! Bill had taken it upon himself to add a little flavor to this adventure and had hidden on the other side of the road and also, brought along his 12 gauge shotgun for a little added sound effects. All I remember when the shotgun went off and what sounded like a heard of buffalo coming out of the road ditch was me running at full speed, Aunt Margie flailing behind me like a rag doll I couldn't shake loose. When we hit the old railroad tie across the road ditch which we used as a walkway to our yard, I am positive Margie never touched the ground until I dropped her on the living room floor on the way to my bedroom to change clothes, not because I had peed all over mine, but because we always dressed for supper in my part of the country!

Uncle Ben...

I lived in a small town in Southeast Missouri called Gideon. It is located about 35 miles North of Blytheville, AR. When I was growing up there was an Air Force Base located at Blytheville that contained the B-52 Bombers that sat "Alert" with their engines running 24/7 ready to defend the United States against Communism during the Cold War years. There was a young man who had just been assigned there around 1962 named Ben Termin. He was a supply technician responsible for materials being shipped in and out of Blytheville AFB. As he became comfortable with the Bootheel area, he began venturing out away from Blytheville AFB to see what else was out there. One weekend he was invited to attend a function somewhere around Kennett Missouri. The exact location is unknown, but the activity was a dance. At this function he spotted a young lady that made his heart go pitty-pat. He could not keep his eyes off of her. Of course his "goofy" gene kicked in order for him to get here attention. I am not sure what he did to accomplish this act, but knowing Ben it was pretty goofy. Goofy or not, it worked and the young lady did notice him and the ritual began. Like a peacock, Ben strutted around the dance floor with his tail feathers glowing! The young lady was Margie Beasley of Gideon, Missouri and she began her own dance that night. Believe me, as her twelve year old nephew in

1962 living with her, I heard about every move that was made. Being not only a nephew, I felt like I was also a good friend, so I listened. For several months I heard more than a twelve year old boy should have to hear about a teenage romance.

Not too many months later they were engaged and a few more months they were married. Being a new Airman in the USAF he did not make much money and Margie was still in high school working part time in a beauty shop. So she left school and they rented a small apartment in Blytheville, AR. I can remember hitch-hiking from Gideon to Portageville to catch the Greyhound bus to Blytheville. I am pretty sure in was like $3.25 for the bus fare.

I spent several weekends with them that summer until they saved enough money to buy a mobile home and placed it in our yard back at Gideon. Not long after they moved in, they bought a new Volkswagen bug, which as a 14 year old boy, was very happy to see. Then, is a few more short months, the baby was due. Now I was about 14 when baby Teresa came along and I was supposed to be the "uninterested" cousin, however, she was a real beauty. I learned babysitting skills pretty quickly and she and I became best friends. She was an exceptional child, she walked early and she talked early. I would like to think it was because of my excellent training skills, but looking back, she might have done all of that even earlier had I not been in her way. Unfortunately God had another plan for her and he took her home to be with him when she was around 2 years old. That was a rough time for all of us. Uncle Ben was stationed in Vietnam when it happened and we had to wait to have the services until he could make his way back home. I was devastated and I just could not imagine what Uncle Ben felt like. Aunt Margie was expecting their second child at the time. Bad time for all involved.

Once this life event passed and Uncle Ben was back in the States they transferred to Texas. They would visit often and Uncle Ben and I grew even closer. We would drive all over Hershell Bell's farm with one of us setting on the front fender of their Volkswagen bug with a shotgun hunting rabbits at night. Uncle Ben sure loved doing that and I would drive him around the farm all night spotting these rabbits in the headlights. One Thanksgiving the family was visiting our house and several of the guys decided to take Uncle Cecil's 1954 Chevy pickup rabbit hunting where we could put a guy on each front fender and three standing in the bed of the truck with the guns pointing over the cab. This was a good idea until Uncle Ben was on the fender and I was standing in the bed of the truck and a rabbit ran out into the field road about a hundred feet in front of us and stopped. We both shot at the same time and there was nothing left of the rabbit but a ball of fur. I am pretty sure Uncle Ben had a few shotgun pellets lodged in his earlobe also, but he never ever said a word about it. I also noticed that he moved from the fender to the back of the truck at the next possible opportunity!

Like I said I was raised by my Grandparents and they were at the age where they didn't really get involved in my extra circular activities. Uncle Ben joined the boy scouts as a leader so I could join as a scout. He also supported and took part in every sporting activity I tried. He was always there to root me on and tell me I could do it if I wanted to.

We were at a high school football game when they lived in Blytheville Arkansas one summer night. As we were leaving the game, we walked around outside of the football stadium when someone kicked a field goal. It went between the goal poles and out into the street where we were walking. Uncle Ben caught the ball and I took off running as hard as I could when he threw the long bomb to me. I caught it and did not stop running until I got to their apartment. We looked for the Blytheville police to stop by the rest of the weekend to arrest us for stealing the football. That was fifty years ago and I still have that ball.

Uncle Ben was killed in a freak accident while riding his Harley Davidson motorcycle a few years back. I think of him often and still miss him to this day…

Uncle Smokey…

I was raised by my granny and Grandpa Beasley, my mother's parents. They had eleven children of their own. When my mother passed away, granny and Grandpa never hesitated to continue raising me, my brother and sister. I was four years old when mom passed and granny and grandpa Beasley had three or four children still at home, one of which was "Uncle Smokey". He was nine years older than me and I looked up to him to set the example, not very smart on my part. My brother and I were living with granny and grandpa Beasley, therefore he and Smokey would fight and wrestle every minute of every day from 1954 through 1956. I hated it when my brother went to live with our dad, because that left me an easy target for Uncle Smokey. He would expend more energy getting me to do his chores than it would have taken to do the chore himself. Although I didn't want to see him harmed, I was very happy when he left for the Air Force. That left me and Aunt Margie at home and I could pretty much out run her. One summer Uncle Smokey came home on leave from the Air Force he was a little low on money, so he thought he would chop a little cotton one Saturday morning to make a few extra dollars. He grabbed a hoe from the back porch and took off across the fields. It was one of those days where the sun was shining and the sky was crystal clear. One hour later an electrical storm came through and it was raining so hard you couldn't see ten feet in front of you. Granny and I was standing on the porch watching it storm and hoping Uncle Smokey had found a safe place to get out of the way of the lightening. In what was the hardest rain and the most lightening of the storm, we heard some one whistling, yes, whistling. We could barely see someone coming down the driveway, it was Uncle Smokey, with hoe handle over his shoulder, like the returning warrior, whistling to the top of his lungs. The next summer Uncle Smokey was home on leave again during cotton chopping time. It was a Saturday and I could go to town when I had finished chopping "Ann's patch", which was a couple of acres. I asked Uncle Smokey if he would give me a hand and he agreed. I was astonished! I thought to myself, the Air Force has been really good for him. I sharpened our hoes and when he got up around 9:00am, he came out to the field to help me. I told him to go over to the other side of the field and start back toward me. We would meet in the middle and I would be off for the day. He went over to the last row and started chopping. When he got to the other end of the row, near the railroad trestle, I saw him stop and was staring up at something. I couldn't see what he was looking at, so I assumed it was something in the trees along the railroad track. I continued chopping over to where he was, only to discover he had chopped one row of cotton, stood his hoe up in a mound of dirt and placed his cap on top of it, pointing toward the trees. He had crossed the trestle and gone to town. I didn't see him until the next day.

Water those Mules...

I've written a little about my Uncle Jerry "Smokey" Beasley. Now I'd like to tell you about his older brother, Uncle Edd Beasley. Uncle Edd's story could be a complete book in itself. From what I was told and the pictures I have seen, Uncle Edd was a striking blonde haired lad that wasn't afraid of women in his younger days, before he was smitten by the Burchell family. Our family, "The Beasleys" moved from Lepanto Arkansas around 1940 and sharecropped for a gentleman named U.S. Holiman. The family lived in one of the twenty three houses located in the field down a gravel road just West of the Cross-Roads Gin. This Gin was located South of Gideon Missouri about three or four miles. These days, if you drive down that gravel road, there is not one sign that anyone ever lived there. No signs of a hustling and bustling community of more than twenty plus families consisting of more than one hundred twenty five people living and working in and around Cross-Roads Gin. How our relatives managed to have ten or eleven children and raise them all to adulthood is beyond my comprehension, but they did it. Near the house where the Beasley family lived was a building called "The Big Barn". This is where they housed the thirty-eight pair of mules used to farm this land. Uncle Edd was around eleven or twelve then and his job was to come in from school and start pumping water for those mules. He would pump for hours with one of those long handled manual pumps every afternoon until the mules were brought in from the field at which time they would drink it half way down in about ten minutes. His dad had him to keep pumping again until he was called in to supper. Uncle Edd said one of the happiest days of his early life was when they brought out a brand new store bought 'Fairbanks-Morse' gas powered water pump. He said he wasn't a very affectionate young man, but, he really loved that pump. And he still had to hand pump until the tank was filled. He reckoned this was not one of his fondest memories. I don't think either family had a vehicle in the 1940s so there travel was somewhat limited. As a young man, the only girls you would see on a regular basis was the families living just across the road or within a mile of them. This was the case for the Beasleys and the Burchells and the Weldons. My Uncle Leon Beasley met and married Leona Burchell in 1946 and that gave Uncle Edd access to Leona's younger sister, Pauline. Being the clever young man he was, took full advantage of that and began courting her before he joined the Air Force in 1948. They were in Love and were married after basic training. Aunt Pauline's mother was very ill at the time and she remained at home to help with her brothers and sisters until her mother passed away in 1949 while Uncle Edd was stationed overseas. While he was stationed in Puerto Rico he was bitten by a centipede on his pointer finger of his right hand. The tip was smaller than the rest of his finger and turned sharply at the last knuckle. This kept him from pointing his finger straght at you. When we would get into trouble, which wasn't often at all, he would get on to us kids for doing something wrong. He would point his finger at us and we couldn't help but laugh because he could not point it straight at us. Afterwards his son, Dan and I would say, "he was pointing at you not me"!

Upon his return from Puerto Rico, Aunt Pauline joined him on their first assignment together in Columbus Ohio. They became a little homesick and come re-enlistment time around 1951 they had had enough of Uncle Sam and they returned to Malden, Missouri where he went to work as a crash rescue specialist at the Malden Air Base. He worked there until the Air Force decided to move the training mission for the Malden Air Base to Enid Oklahoma. Uncle Edd said he did not relocate with the unit because he "didn't know anyone in Oklahoma". At this time my Uncle Leon was operating a dragline all around the bootheel of Missouri. Uncle Edd went to work with him as an oiler keeping the dragline lubricated. He took this opportunity to learn how to operate the dragline from his brother and soon he moved from oiler to operator. Once He helped move a dragline to Southern Illinois and was offered a operator position in the strip mining business. He decided against that option and returned to Gideon. Times were hard and jobs were scarce. He worked at the box plant in Gideon and said he worked fifty-five hrs per week for twenty seven dollars. One of his fellow workers said "we should have to wear striped uniforms to work here". Guess times were hard all over. He didn't last but a few months at the box plant.

Said he had to be outside and he began a career operating the dragline. Uncle Leon and Aunt Leona moved to Southern Illinois to work the strip mines and remained there until they both passed away. Uncle Edd worked all around SouthEast Missouri, SouthWest Arkansas and Southern Illinois. He tried to keep his family stable and they lived over on six ditch near Risco Missouri, over on the sand road just Northeast of Campbell Missouri, and then into Campbell. They worked around Southern Illinois for a few years until they moved back to the Missouri bootheel. I even worked with him for a while in 1970 in Tchula, Mississippi while my need bride, Colette, lived with Pauline and their kids. They tried a short period of time in Dyersburg, Tennessee. However they couldn't stay away and returned to the bootheel area. Once all of their children had graduated from high school they had worked all around the local area, they ended up in Clarkton Missouri and that is where he lives today at eighty two years young. Aunt Pauline, "Polly" went to live with our Lord in 2004. They had five children, Danny, Sue, Pam, Emily, and Kenny. Kenny was a special needs baby and although the Lord only saw fit to let them have him thirteen years, he will live in our hearts forever.

The Beasley brothers marrying the Burchell sisters began a lifelong relationship. We have celebrated this relationship with a B & B family reunion for over forty years. Currently held at Sam A. Baker park, weekend of the fourth of July. Stop in and join us!

I had graduated and left home to find my fame and fortune, (still looking by the way). I was home visiting my Grandparents one weekend when the phone rang and it was Uncle Edd. Apparently he and Aunt Pauline had some sort of domestic disagreement and he had "ran away from home". He asked if I would come to the community of McGuire and pick him up. It was around 8:00pm when I turned into Mr Battles custard stand and all of the lights were out. There was Uncle Edd setting at the picnic table with his suitcase by his side. I said well, I guess he HAS ran away from home at forty years old. I picked him up and we took off toward Malden and made it all the way to "The Long Branch" bar. Both of us were pretty fair pool players at the time and we met a couple of guys who begged to differ! After 2 or 3 hours Uncle Edd and I left the Long Branch with about three cases of beer that those gentlemen "donated" to the cause. He returned home with me, got a lecture from his mother, and I took him back home the next morning.

Uncle Edd told me of a time around 1945 when the Beasleys lived in a small community known as Little Walnut where my Grandpa rented 160 acres. Had his own pair of mules and a small tractor. Life was looking up for them back then. For no known reason, Grandpa sold everything, packed up the family and moved to Michigan. That was not a brilliant plan. He said he can remember Grandpa buying a 1943 automobile, loading his children, Deanner, Edd, Jean, Ann, Smokey, Little Bill, and Margie into the car with everything they owned and returning to Gideon. I suppose we all had to chase our dreams, good or bad.

There are many more stories I could tell you about Uncle Edd, but to me his story is that I would show up at his door from the time I was five years old until last week and was welcomed in like a brother. I spent most of my life trying to model my family life after his. Although not perfect, it was perfect enough for me.

When I met you baby…

I graduated from Gideon High School in 1968, moved to Dennison-Sherman Texas to live with my Aunt Margie Beasley Termin. Her and Uncle Ben Termin were stationed there in the Air Force. I went to work for Levis-Strauss. I knew pretty quickly that factory work was not for me, so I saw an advertisement in the Dallas TX newspaper for a training course to learn how to work on computers. They weren't very sophisticated in 1968, so I was sure that this was what I wanted. There was never any talk around my house about college simply because we didn't have the money to go and I wasn't smart enough to apply for any type of grant or student loans. I was raised that you finished high school and went right into the work force.

My Uncle Ben's father lived in Dallas so he and Margie drove me down to Dallas where I enrolled in the computer school. They even found me a job to help me pay for the course. I worked in the shipping department of Texlite Sign Company located at the airport. We built wooden crates used for shipping large lighted signs primarily used at gas stations around the country. I did this for a few months over the summer for 1968. Although I hadn't spent one minute in a computer class, I had managed to buy a Gold, 1965 Chevy Super Sport to strut around in and strut I did. I remember wondering how I was going to pay those $95.00 payments. Thinking I was homesick, I packed up my Chevy and headed to St Louis to make my fortune.

I moved in with my cousin, Wayman Baker and his wife who lived in Edmundson, Missouri, just outside of the St Louis airport. I quickly went to work in a foundry for a week, Nestle's Cocoa for a week, and even tried working at the Fisher Body plant for a few months. Third shift was interfering with my social life way too much in 1969. My cousin, Carmelita, introduced me to a guy named Danny Woods who worked for Kelly Springfield tire. He took me under his wing and taught me the trade of Brakes, and frontend alignment. I had taken these classes while in high school. Those two years of attending the Vo-Tec at Malden, Missouri were about to pay off. Thanks again to Vernon Tolbert for convincing me to hang in there that someday it will be beneficial. He was right. I worked there a year and was promoted to service manager and moved to another store in Florissant, Missouri.

One of my good friends from High School, Loren Stephens, lived across the river in Bethalto, Illinois at that time. I decided to drive over one Sunday and visit him and his wife Charlotte. Looking for something to do, we decided to play a game of football. We went over to the next little village of Meadowbrook where there was some guys playing in the church lot. One of the guys playing with us was the preacher's son, Steve Woodfin. We had been playing for an hour or so when Steve's younger sister, Lynn, came by to tell him it was supper time. She had a girl with her that caught my eye. I found out later her name was Colette Gregory. There was no doubt in my mine, she was the one. I could not keep my eyes off of her. I am sure it was obvious, but I didn't care, she was cuter than a speckled pup. After doing a little investigating, I was waiting in her driveway when she returned home from church that night. For the next few weeks I pursued her like a beagle chasing a rabbit. Have you ever been to a rodeo and watched the "cutting" horses? Well that was me. She couldn't make a move to the left or the right that I didn't cut her off. Obviously, at first, she didn't see our future as clearly as I did. I even had to dust off my bible and make a few early morning trips from St Louis, Missouri to Meadowbrook, Illinois and attend church just to see her. This was about 70 miles one way and after all, gas was 24.9 cents per gallon! A fella could go broke courting like this. She contracted pneumonia in December of 1969 and was admitted to the hospital in Alton, Illinois, probably from trying to outrun me without a jacket. I caught her at her weakest point and proposed marriage in the hospital. In a drug induced state she agreed and we were married 7 June 1970.

When we married, I was working at the Brown Shoe factory in Bernie, Missouri. About a year before the wedding, Colette's father had a heart attack and passed away. We sort of lost momentum for a while, but being young, we bounced back and continued forward. At that point the financing of the wedding fell on Colette and I. We were fortunate enough to have the preacher's wife make her dress and all of her friends helped out, we made it through it. Unfortunately, there was no honeymoon. We moved into a duplex in Malden, MO.

From that day forth she has been by my side through 43 years of marriage. Twenty plus years in the U.S. Air Force traveling from Las Vegas, NV to Lakenheath, England. She remained in the States taking care of the children while I took a side trip to Korea for a year. There were some pretty lean years and our move here to Ohio last June was our 35th move since we married and she was there with me every step. Hopefully she will stay with me now, just to see how it turns out!

When the hog ate my little brother...

Once upon a time there were two sisters. The older one, let's call her Carmelita with her dark red hair and big wide grin. She was not afraid to talk anyone into anything! Then there was her younger sister, let's call her Carolyn. She had that sheepish grin and was covered with freckles from head to toe. I am sure she was the first one that Carmelita convinced to try everything. Just for the fun of it let's give them the last name of Baker.

Carmelita was around seven years old and Carolyn was about five in 1949 when they lived just a few miles outside of Gideon, Missouri. Their daddy was a sharecropper and he spent very long days in the fields working the farm while their momma spent most of the day either cleaning the house, washing the clothes, or preparing the meals. With no video games to play on, this left Carmelita and Carolyn plenty of time to be outside, rain or shine or snow. Two little girls playing inside on a snowing day, screaming and yelling just wasn't going to happen, so it was outside for them. Although these two girls had free run of the farm, they knew right from wrong and what was out of bounds for them. Sometimes the right and wrong line got a little blurry but, they generally stayed on the right side of it, for the most part. There were times when Carolyn found herself on the wrong side of the line with Carmelita's guidance. As they grew older and Carolyn got a little wiser she learned to drag their little brother, let's call him Wayman, in to take the blame when needed. He was probably already crying about something anyway, so it didn't really matter.

One cold winter day Carmelita noticed the barn door was open to the loft and it was full of hay. She really wanted to go up and play in the hayloft, but couldn't get the big barn door open, even with Carolyn's help. The only other way to get into the loft was through the pigpen at the other end of the barn. Carmelita tried her best to talk Carolyn into crawling through the fence and running across the pigpen where she could then open the barn door and let Carmelita in so they could play in the barn loft. Carolyn was too afraid of the big sow and thought if she went into the pigpen, the big sow would eat her up. Carmelita tried her best to tell Carolyn that that old sow wouldn't hurt a flea and that she was just being a big baby about it. Carolyn said "why don't you go open the door"? Carmelita explained that she was too big to fit through the boards in the fence or she would be over there in a flash. She just about had Carolyn convinced to make the trip across the pigpen when around the corner came Wayman, decked out in overalls unsnapped at the bottom with a "loaded" diaper hanging partially out of one leg. Carmelita and Carolyn saw this as the perfect opportunity. They both went to work on Wayman and quickly convinced him how much fun they would have in the hayloft if he would open the door for them. Wayman was nearing the end of his "terrible twos" and feared nothing. He slide under the fence and began the stroll over to the other side of the pigpen grinning from ear to ear, when suddenly the big sow that had been rooting around at the other end of the pigpen caught a whiff of Wayman's "loaded" diaper and it smelled to her like an apple pie fresh out of the oven. She headed toward him grunting and snorting. The girls saw this and Carolyn thinking the sow was going to eat Wayman, crawled through the fence and ran towards him also. Carmelita was actually hoping the hog would eat him, but decided it would be hard to explain to the judge and began yelling for Wayman to hurry to the other side. Wayman finally saw the old sow headed his was and took one last dive for the fence, rolled right under it to safety. Suddenly Carolyn found herself with the sow between her and the fence and thought this was the end. She just kenw she was going to be eaten, when the old sow turned to see what Carmelita was screaming about, Carolyn darted to the left jumped and placed one foot on the lower board of the fence, climbed over the fence and was safe by Wayman's side. All of a sudden it came to Carolyn, why didn't Carmelita climbed over the fence earlier instead of trying to crawl through it? This was a turning point in Carolyn's life. From this point on Carmelita had a tough time getting her to fall of those types of stunts. Wayman was safe, but still screaming like the hog ate his leg off. He and Carolyn went into the barn only to find out they were too short to reach the door handle and couldn't let Carmelita in. So with that, Carolyn and Wayman climbed up to the hayloft and played for hours while Carmelita sat playing with two corncobs just outside of the pigpen…

Who did it….

When I was about six and my sister, (Sissie) was about nine years old we were playing in the back yard. She would always try to get me to play with dolls, but I just couldn't bring myself to do it, even as a small boy. However, I could talk her into doing almost anything because she had no one else to play with.

We always started our day out excited to get outside and play. One day we were playing with cars in the back yard I had the great idea to build a tunnel for our cars to drive through. The ground in our yard was so hard, we couldn't scrape up enough dirt to build a hill big enough to make a tunnel through it. We looked around for something to use and I ran across wicker clothes basket out by the clothes line in the back yard. It was perfect, but, Sissie said it was Granny's clothes basket for brining in the laundry from the clothesline. I told her we were just gonna borrow it for a while and we would put it back. We took it and it was perfect except for one thing, when we drove the cars into the tunnel, we couldn't reach them to get them out. I talked Sis into cutting the bottom out of the basket so we can access the cars from the top. When we finished playing, we placed the basket back by the clothesline and dropped the bottom we had cut out down in the basket. Once Granny gathered the clothes, filled the basket and went to pick it up, the bottom and all of her clothes hit the ground. Her response was, "Boy (which was my nickname), what have you done"? I jumped up from the ground and ran over to see what she was talking about. With the most surprised look on my face I could come up with, I confessed, "Sissie did it"!

A few days later Sis and I were playing around in the back yard where I had designed an excellent snare out of a piece of clothesline. We were using it for big game hunting in the chicken coop. I had it sticking through the chicken wire with the loop on the ground inside the coop. We had dropped some corn in the loop and were waiting for the big game to come by. Soon two big fat hens came over near us, scratching the ground and looking for food. They spotted the corn and both went after it, with each hen having a foot in the noose, I gave it a big jerk and low and behold, I caught both of them. With that, the two hens went crazy and began to squawk. It sounded like we were killing them. Granny came running out the back door yelling, "what on earth have you youngins' done now". With our backs to Granny, she couldn't see who was holding the clothesline snare, so I quickly handed it to Sis and wrapped it around her arm so she couldn't let go, jumped to my feet and shouted, "Sissie did it"!

She had avoided playing with me for a few days so I was in the backyard alone with a hand full of broom straws catching grub worms from the holes in our yard. How many of you have done that before? One of our favorite past times back then. Find those perfectly round holes in your yard, drop a broom straw (must be straight), into the hole and watch the grub worm start pushing it out of the hole. When he gets a good grip on the straw and is near the top of the hole, snatch on the straw and out he comes, excellent fishing bait. Anyway, I've got like three or four straws going at one time, I am slaying those rascals when Granny comes off the back porch screaming at me, "Boy, look what you have done now". She is carrying her best broom with a very large chunk of straws cut out of it. I knew I had used the old broom from the smoke house, cause I knew how mad Granny would get if I used her new broom, so I jumped to my feet in an attempt to explain my way out of this one when she showed me a note attached to the broom written by a small child that said, "Boy did it"! I saw sissie out of the corner of my eye hiding around the corner of the chicken house, snickering…

You can't do that...

I just had a great Christmas week with my kids and my grandkids. After they left to return to their homes and it was quite again, I began thinking about how my grandkids were so limited in what they could do compared to when I was their ages. Looking back at what a privilege it was growing up in the bootheel of Southeast Missouri, in and around Gideon in the 1960s.

I played out in the yard about a half mile outside of Gideon and my Granny had no fear of me being snatched out of the yard by some pervert. I'm sure she looked out of the living room window occasionally to see me playing in the dirt driveway with my tractors and cars. I built more highways in that yard than Eisenhower built Interstates. There were overpasses, underpasses, and rivers to contend with in my highway systems. I ran big tonka trucks over hotwheel cars and no one was ever even scratched. I was a master road constructor at age 8 and thought nothing of it. Later I progressed to playing basketball on a peach basket nailed to an old cable spool my Grandpa brought home, or batting rocks in a world series ballgame. I batted so many, I thought I should have emptied that driveway of rocks.

At around twelve years old I remember hitchhiking from Gideon to Clarkton, or Gideon to Malden, or Gideon to Portageville and never even considered some depraved lunatic picking me up and harming me in anyway. I'm sure there were sickos out there, but I just didn't know or care about them. I walked everywhere I went either alone or with friends. We played all over town in every yard or vacant lot there was. We drank after each other out of everyone's water hoses. Our parents didn't know where we were most of the time and as long as we were home before the street lights came on, we were OK. Once Ronnie Lowery and I were gathering soda bottles to cash in for a couple of full ones when we flipped the bike we were riding and a broken bottle cut my wrist. Ronnie took me up to Doctor Hopkins clinic where his mother was a nurse. Doc stitched me up and sent me home with a bill for $3.00. Some of those hot summer nights we would go home, eat supper, and head right back outside to play hide and seek all over town.

I hitch-hiked up until I was sixteen and my Aunt Margie and Uncle Ben bought a Volkswagen bug. Once I managed to pass my driver's test, they let me drive it from time to time. Even after I started driving, they didn't know where I was and wasn't too worried about my safety. It was simply a different time in History. I really hate it because my grandkids are missing what I had.

My Grandkids, unlike me can't go outside like I could because there are "predators" out there ready to grab them and do God knows what to them. If they are able to go outside they have to stay near the door and report in every half hour or so to let the parents know they were OK. The very thing the WWII generation fought for has slipped right through our hands. The sad part is that it wasn't our enemies that have taken it, it was our own thirst for Getting rid of God from our schools, Government buildings, and trying to stop the spread of Christianity. Political Correctness has somehow given free reign for drug dealers to stand on street corners and spread their poison, yet let a Christian man stand on the street corner and try to spread the word of God and he can now be arrested. Prayer has been removed from the schools, sports events, and now even the military chaplins can't talk about God in their services. What has this got to do with our Grandkids not being able to play outside? If you can't figure it out, then maybe you are part of the problem.

Sorry, someone must have brought a soapbox into the room.

We have replaced what we can't allow our grandkids to do with Electronic gadgets that keep them safely in their rooms where we don't have to worry about them. They have access to world of information through the internet, but they seem to be getting less smart. They are losing their social skills by not being outside and interacting with the rest of the world. Try to have a conversation with your grandkid with their parents around. You ask them a question and the parent answers it. I think they are afraid to the child speak because of the amount of disrespect that comes flowing from their mouths. Again, no social skills and no filters.

My advice if you want to let your grandkids have a little of what you had growing up is to let them play outside even if you have to hide in the bushes and lookout for the perverts so they won't have to worry about it. They will remember you fondly as the one that took the time to give them some of what you had.

Made in the USA
Monee, IL
04 January 2022